To Jenny From

Kelly

EASY GLAMOUR

The Black Woman's Definitive Guide to Beauty and Style

EASY GLAMOUR

The Black Woman's Definitive Guide to Beauty and Style

Barbara Walden
with Vicki Lindner

Line Drawings by Lamont O'Neal

Color Photographs by Wendy V. Townsend

WILLIAM MORROW AND COMPANY, INC.

New York

Library of Congress Cataloging in Publication Data

Walden, Barbara D
  Easy glamour.

    Includes index.
    1. Beauty, Personal. 2. Cosmetics. 3. Women,
Black—Health and hygiene. 4. Walden, Barbara.
5. Actors—United States—Biography. I. Lindner, Vicki
1944–   joint author. II. Title.
RA778.W17   646.7′2′088042   80-29249
ISBN 0-688-00416-4

Printed in the United States of America

    3 4 5 6 7 8 9 10

Book design by Lydia Link

Acknowledgments

Consultant for the skin chapter was Dr. Robert Auerbach, New York City. I would also like to acknowledge Dr. Bedford Shelmire, Jr.'s excellent book, *The Art of Looking Younger.*

I would like to thank Jerry Munchweiler, one of Hollywood's outstanding makeup artists, who shared some of his secrets with me for the makeup chapter.

My special thanks to Barbara Morris of B.J. Bubbles, Inc., New York (and her staff), for gracious assistance with the chapter on hair and the styles she created for the photographs. I would also like to thank Art Dyson for his valuable information and comments. Other consultants were Daniel Mitchell, Hal Truesdale, Elizabeth D. Cunningham, and Ralph Holbrook Micks, my personal hairdresser in Santa Monica, California.

Consultants for the hands and feet chapter were Donna LeClair of Fortune in Beverly Hills, Jacqueline Bullock of the Aida Thibiant Salon, Beverly Hills, and Joy Ercolano of the B.J. Bubbles Salon, New York.

Finally, thanks to the women who modeled for the color photographs: Ronke Adefope, Barbara Ash, Jennifer Butler, Chachi, Lynn Ferrel, Louise Jones, Polly Roberts, Mitoka Singletary, Karen Wadkins, Bhetty Waldron, and Maritza Williamson.

Special Thanks

To my dear mother, family, and Dan Raeburn, whose help and guidance made it all possible;

to Maria Guarnaschelli, my editor, who had faith in me;

to Penny Riley for her research;

to Bhetty Waldron for her generous support all during the project;

to Vicki Lindner for her hard work;

to all the cosmetic buyers throughout the country for their confidence;

and to my dear friends Chez Marie, Bill and Gussie Kermin, Sam and Ethel Katz, and Abe and Muriel Lipsey, whose love was always there

Contents

Introduction: The Barbara Walden Story   1

1 Glamour-Right Skin Care   **15**

2 The Barbara Walden Complete Makeup   **48**

3 Creating Good Hair   **88**

4 Dressin' Up   **142**

5 Beautiful Hands and Feet   **175**

6 Star Quality: Becoming Conscious of the Total You   **193**

Index   **203**

Introduction
The Barbara Walden Story

When I was ten I had a knockdown, drag-out battle with my brother, whose skin is lighter than mine. "Barbara, you're black!" he shouted. At that time, more than thirty years ago, *black* was a derogatory word, and I thought it was the nastiest name I'd ever been called. Totally devastated, I burst into tears and screamed back, "I am *not* black!" My mother overheard this quarrel, took me by the hand, and led me to the mirror, where I saw my undeniably dark face staring at me. "Yes, Barbara," she said, "you are black. You are my beautiful black girl and don't you ever think differently." It was due to my wise mother that I grew up proud to be black.

In the sixties, when everyone proclaimed "black is beautiful," it wasn't new to me. In the Walden family we had always been taught to be proud of what we were and to hold our heads up high. When I was criticized by some of my friends for not wearing my hair naturally in an Afro, I told them, "I don't have to wear a sign on my back. I *know* I was born black, and I've felt beautiful all of my life."

We Waldens were never allowed to admit we couldn't do something because of our color. My mother refused to acknowledge the power of racial prejudice. When I was a teenager I applied to a modeling school in New York City. The school rejected me because I was black. This was the first time in my life I had really felt the effects of racism, and I couldn't bring myself to tell my mother why the school had turned me down. Instead, I told her I'd been rejected because I was too short. She set me to work doing stretching exercises. A fraction of an inch taller, I applied again. This time I told her the school had probably rejected me because I was too fat and clumsy. My mother put me on a diet and made me practice walking with a book on my head until I was dizzy. Finally, the director of the modeling school gave up and let me in; she must have realized I would keep coming back until she did. All the time I was sure my mother knew the real reason the school would not admit me, but she refused to recognize race as a barrier that determination could not overcome. She trained me to fight for what I wanted and never to settle for less than I deserved.

That advice often led me to defy my mother as well. When I was sixteen I began sneaking out of the house to travel to New York, where I had gotten a job in a Greenwich Village nightclub dancing in a very brief costume. I used to tell my mother I was going ice skating in Rockefeller Center. Unfortunately, I made the mistake of telling my best girl friend. She in turn disclosed the information to her mother, who promptly told mine. One evening I looked out into the audience and saw—guess who?—my mother, with the world's most furious expression on her face. Modern dancing in scanty attire was not what she had in mind for her beautiful black daughter. I raced off the stage and back to my dressing room, and ran right smack into my mother who must have leaped over every table in the place to get there so fast. She demanded that I get dressed immediately. Meanwhile the owner, who had believed me when I'd said I was twenty-one, was also frantic. They were all in such a hurry to get me out of there that I never got paid for that evening. My mother later told me that the dancing lessons she had been giving me were to teach me how to be graceful—and that's all!

After high school my parents sent me to business college, and after two unhappy years I rebelled. I was determined to go to Hollywood instead and pursue my dream of becoming an actress and dancer, though at that time the few parts for blacks were scarcely starring roles. Because I arrived in Hollywood with an "attitude," I had a difficult time. I would not accept any role I felt was derogatory to my race, and that meant that very few were open to me.

Twice I said "no thanks" to the part of Elizabeth Taylor's maid. The first maid's role was in *Raintree County* with Liz and Montgomery Clift. I turned it down because I was expected to shuffle around drawling "Yassum" and "Nossuh." "I don't mind playing the part of a maid," I told the director, "but at least let me talk like a human being. I never heard *anyone* talk like that!" He didn't agree, and we went our separate ways. Later, the black actress who eagerly accepted the role thanked me for refusing it. According to her, my spirited protest had made a few small waves. The director had changed "Yassum" and "Nossuh" to "Yes, ma'am" and "No, sir."

Next I turned down the part of Elizabeth Taylor's handmaiden in "Cleopatra." The producer had seen my photographs and was excited about using me in the movie, a multimillion-dollar extravaganza to be filmed in Europe. My agent was also thrilled, and I tried to psych myself into accepting the role. On the way out to the studio, my agent repeated that this was a fabulous opportunity, and I felt fully prepared to accept the part. When I got to the studio, and looked over the script, something deep inside me resisted. "Don't you read your history books?" I said to the director. "Cleopatra was a brown woman! If you had Elizabeth Taylor playing *my* handmaiden, you'd have it right. There's no *way* I can do this part." No one could believe his ears. The director and producer went into a huddle. "Didn't she know what part it was?" they asked my embarrassed agent, who was in a rage. Once outside the studio door, she dropped me like a hot potato for wasting her time, and I took the bus back home. It was impossible to explain to her what had taken place in me—that I had gone in good faith, but when I got to the studio I couldn't be Elizabeth Taylor's maid and still be Barbara!

I soon acquired a reputation. Other black actresses and actors, as well as the producers and directors, began to regard me as a troublemaker. My black friends accused me of putting on airs and worried that, thanks to me, the movie industry would soon refuse to give blacks any roles at all. I had no friends, but I couldn't change. That's the way I am. I landed very few parts, but I did get the ear of the press. "Here's an unknown young actress who's determined to do things her way." In the press I was always referred to as "That Unknown." I was lonely and frustrated. Sometimes I'd say to myself, "Okay, I'll just accept whatever role they're offering," but when the time came to compromise myself, I couldn't deny the pride I'd been raised to feel in myself and my people.

Even when I did find an acceptable role, I'd continue to open my big mouth and agitate for changes. I told off the director of *Carmen Jones*. "You have a heavyweight championship fight scene here, and you have only blacks in the audience," I said. "That's not true to life. Not only blacks go to see a major fight!" I also helped found the Beverly Hills–Hollywood chapter of the NAACP, and wrote letters to everyone at the top, including President Kennedy, to urge the film industry to represent American blacks in a positive way. Recently I played a bit part in the film *Car Wash,* and the director was black, I saw blacks in starring roles, and blacks doing technical jobs—things that were not possible when I was first starting out. I knew times had really changed, and I like to think that, in my own small way, I contributed to some of those changes.

After the *Cleopatra* fiasco I got a more sympathetic agent. He told me that Universal Pictures was holding a beauty contest to choose seven young girls for the parts of Satan's Seven Sinners in a new Mickey Rooney film, *The Private Lives of Adam and Eve.* He said he was sorry that he couldn't enter me because he knew I would be rejected; a black girl in a studio beauty contest was so unheard of, he felt, that I wouldn't stand a chance, and he didn't want to subject me to the embarrassment of being turned down. Then I remembered what my mother had always taught me. I told my agent, "I'm qualified. That's all that matters. I'm just as pretty as any other girl who will enter that contest. If you don't take me, I'll go myself." I remember my agent's resigned smile when he said, "If that's what you want, I'll take you."

To my agent's surprise (but not to mine) I was chosen to be one of Satan's Seven Sinners out of 350 contestants, along with a Japanese girl and five white girls. I still remember that triumphant day. That night I sat at home and flipped from channel to channel on the television set, watching myself on all the major networks being interviewed and talked about in depth. One reporter said that history had been made because a black girl had been chosen over more than three hundred white girls in one of the largest beauty contests ever held at a major studio. In the weeks that passed, while we waited for shooting to begin on the film, there were newspaper and radio interviews, and an exclusive feature interview with Associated Press columnist Jim Bacon that ran in major newspapers throughout the world. Letters, telegrams, and phone calls poured in congratulations. It was one of the most exciting times of my life. I felt it would be smooth sailing from then on, but smooth it wasn't.

First, the Universal studio got an angry phone call from its headquarters in New York saying, "Have you people gone crazy out there?" When we began to shoot the film, I found there was a conspiracy to keep my appearance in it down to a minimum. The wardrobe mistress would spend so much time perfecting my costume that when I emerged I'd discover the scene I was dressed for had already been shot. When there was a dancing scene, I was kept as far away from Mickey Rooney as possible. The other Sinners would be waltzing with him seductively, and I'd be off to the side, doing a solo. I was forbidden actually to touch the star in a massage scene. Finally, *Playboy* came out to the coast to do a feature on the film and shoot photos of the sexy Seven Sinners. Now I had a hell of a figure in those days if I do say so myself. It could stand up against any woman's, including those of the other Six Sinners. But *Playboy*, which eventually became a very liberal magazine, did not want to include me in the photos because I was black. The director tried to defend me. "If Barbara Walden is not in the feature, *Playboy* can't shoot it," he announced, but in the end he was overruled by the head office, and *Playboy* shot a photo spread with only Six Sinners in it.

At that point I had taken almost as much as I could take. I called my agent and told him I was walking out. He pleaded with me to stay and finish the film, because if I left, I would be playing right into the hands of the studio bosses, who had been against me from the beginning. I did decide to stay and not give in to the studio's manipulative tactics. I ended up having several dance scenes in the finished film. But on the whole, what had begun as a wonderful opportunity turned out to be a disappointing experience.

MY NEW CAREER

When I first went to Hollywood, my family helped support my acting career. Thanks to my parents' generous help I was in a good position to turn down undesirable parts because I knew that even if I didn't work I wasn't going to starve. About four years after I'd moved to the West Coast, however, I told my parents I couldn't come home for Christmas. They were hurt and said, "If your exciting life in California is so important to you that you don't need us at Christmas, perhaps you don't need us for anything anymore." After that I was on my own financially; but I was determined to maintain my security blanket so I could remain independent and accept only those roles I wanted to play. I went to work for a company that made a household product called Dabit. I began demonstrating this product from door to door. I hired people and trained them, and formed sales crews. This supplied me with important business training. Later, when I wanted to start my own business, I knew exactly how to do it.

A few years later, I began to create my own cosmetics. At that time there was no makeup for the black woman, and nothing the movie studios used on me looked right. The pancake foundations made for white skins turned my skin purple or a grotesque chalky shade. Often the makeup artist on the set would try to make my skin look lighter or different—with disastrous results. The makeup men sometimes told me I looked fine without makeup because they didn't have the slightest idea what products to use on me. My hair was another problem. The minute the hot studio lights and humidity hit me, my careful hot-combing and set would revert to a short, curly natural, and naturals were not in fashion then. I would have to hot-comb and curl my hair again before the scene could be shot, which took valuable time.

Finally, I decided to attack this problem myself. I hired a chemist, and we began to design a foundation especially for my skin. Because I had an art background and painted in my spare time, I had excellent intuitions about color. I could see that there were orange undertones in my brown skin. I'd urge the chemist, "Mix some orange with that brown." I drove the poor man crazy, but with my usual determination I persisted to get what I wanted and no less. After much trial and error, I created a sheer foundation that brought out the glowing undertones in my skin—a beautiful makeup I could wear on the set or on the street.

When I proudly began to wear my custom-made foundation, my black friends said, "You look great! What do you have on your skin?" I began to give samples of my makeup away. After innumerable requests and as many pleased reactions, I suspected I had a product, and an idea, I could sell. I knew existing cosmetic companies didn't bother to make anything special for the black woman. My makeup, I thought, could be one of the first cosmetic lines for black women to appear. A good friend, Dan Raeburn, and I each invested $350 in my new business. I worked with the chemist to expand my line of products, and I began to market them door-to-door in the Watts section of Los Angeles.

Everyone told me I was out of my mind. Women with low incomes, they said, will never buy cosmetics. Yet not one lady shut the door in my face. They invited me into their living rooms, listened to what I had to say, and bought my products when they could. Those same ladies are still my customers, and my heart belongs to them. They come into the major department stores where my products are sold now, put their arms around me, and say, "You were in my house!" From them I learned that most black women did not realize how beautiful they were. Because they never saw their images in television advertisements, in movies, or in fashion magazines, they had been brainwashed to believe only white skin, thin lips, and slim noses were beautiful. They disliked their noses and their lips, and many, until they met me, had bought no cosmetics at all or only those that made their skin look lighter and their lips less conspicuous. Everywhere I went my message was: We *are* beautiful! We have beautiful skin, beautiful full lips, and beautiful noses. Let's make the most of what we have.

I began to approach department stores with my products. By then I was sure even women with limited means were willing to buy cosmetics that would enhance their beauty. The stores turned me down flat. I retaliated by opening my own beauty clinic on Crenshaw Boulevard. I telephoned all the women I knew and invited women's clubs and organizations to my beautiful blue clinic for makeovers. I gave skin analyses, wardrobe advice, helped my customers restyle their hair, and hired makeup artists to do their faces. I always directed my marketing efforts at the average woman—not actresses and entertainers. Gradually a new clientele—professional women and the wives of professional men—began to visit my clinic, too. One of my first customers was Ethel Bradley, the wife of the mayor of Los Angeles, who remains an enthusiastic Barbara Walden fan to this day.

One of the very first new products I developed was a failure-proof hairstyling gel which I needed for my own unmanageable hair. I worked hard with my chemist to get that product right. I was always the guinea pig. I would set my hair with our latest formula, go to a dinner on Saturday night with gorgeous smooth curls, and by midnight find my hair looking like a wet chicken's. The next morning I'd be right back at the laboratory to redo the formula.

When I finally had a perfect version, I began to sell the product myself with great success. I then called on the buyer of the Thrifty Drug Store chain in Los Angeles, but he turned me down. "We can't sell a seven-fifty product to black women in a chain store like Thrifty's," he said. I said, "It can be done." I went back to my office and called that buyer's boss, and set up a new meeting. This time I went armed with sales reports from my clinic.

The big boss looked at my figures and said, "I think we might be able to do business." That sentence took me from where I was then to where I am today. Thrifty gave me a big purchase order that kept me licking labels and pasting them on jars for two solid weeks.

BIG DECISION

When I began my business I thought I could continue to work as an actress. I considered the cosmetic business an alternative career and had no intention of giving up my real ambition. As my business expanded, I continued to keep in touch with my agent and go out for parts that appealed to me. Soon my products, now in beautiful packages, were also in the Broadway Department Stores. Finally, Joseph Magnin, a luxury department store in San Francisco, agreed to open my line.

I arrived in San Francisco three days before the opening to promote my cosmetics on television talk shows. I was interviewed by the local newspapers, and major advertisements had been placed in all of them. On opening day the product line was a huge success. All the store executives were overwhelmed by the public's positive reaction. On the third day of the promotion campaign, I received a call at my hotel from a director in Hollywood I had worked with. He said he was doing a TV pilot that had a terrific part in it for me. He told me that the pilot could eventually become a regular series. How soon could I return to Los Angeles?

I told him I'd fly back first thing in the morning. I then called Marvin Frank, the Magnin buyer, and told him I would not be in the store the next day because I had just been offered a fabulous role in a TV pilot and I was returning to Los Angeles the next day. There was complete silence for a moment, then he said, "How wonderful! But when you leave tomorrow morning, make sure you've packed up every piece of your cosmetics so you can take them all back to L.A. If you walk out of this store, every one of your products goes with you."

"You've got to be kidding," I said.

"No," he replied. "I'm as serious as my name is Marvin Frank. We've swamped this city with ads, and you've been on television promising you'll be in our store promoting your cosmetics and meeting the customers. If one woman hires a babysitter to keep her child while she comes to Joseph Magnin to meet you, and you're not here, to me she's a victim of false advertising."

It was a tremendous decision to make. I paced the floor of my hotel. The Joseph Magnin account was a prestigious one and I had worked hard to get it. I thought about the letters I received from customers and all the women I had helped improve their looks and recognize their beauty. I thought about the TV role, a meaningful part I really wanted to do, and the possibility that the pilot would become a full-fledged series and make me a star. I did not say a word to anyone all night long. It was a choice I had to make myself.

The next morning I arrived at the store when it opened. Marvin was waiting for me. "Shall we pack?" he asked.

"Don't say *pack* to me," I replied. *"Pack* is a dirty word. No, we don't pack. In fact, when this week is over you'll be asking me to ship more of my products to your store. We'll be *unpacking* Barbara Walden cosmetics for years to come." That morning I knew I was where I really wanted to be, and I've never regretted my decision. I knew then I would stick with my business, even if it meant giving up acting for good.

CHICAGO TRIUMPH

I went back to Los Angeles after the Magnin opening and soon sold our line to Chicago's biggest department store—Carson, Pirie, Scott, and Company. This was in the sixties, a time of serious social unrest in Chicago. Blacks were angry and setting fires to numerous department stores in the city. Carson, Pirie, Scott wanted to prove to the black community that their store had its interests in mind. They wanted to bring in a line of black cosmetics, produced and operated by a black person who was not just a front figure but really involved. My partner and I went to Chicago to talk to the buyer. She asked how much money she needed to spend to bring the line into two of their stores. Dan and I looked at each other; we were both ready to say five thousand dollars because that's how much our first big store, Joseph Magnin, had spent. Before I could answer, the buyer said, "Well, I think we'll bring twenty thousand dollars of cosmetics into our downtown store, and ten thousand dollars' worth into our suburban store." We nearly fell off our chairs. All I could think about was how hard it was going to be to stick labels on thirty thousand dollars' worth of our products in two months.

When opening week arrived, my schedule was unbelievable. Four makeup artists and I flew in to do the promotion. A limousine picked us up at the airport. There were flowers in every room of my hotel suite. I was interviewed on two or three television and radio shows a day, and the entire press turned out at a special luncheon for me at the Arts Club of Chicago. Eight windows of the downtown store carried pictures of me and displays of my product. The black community began buying my cosmetics before the promotion actually began. The buyer placed another order immediately. "I think we have a tiger by the tail," she said. The night after the line opened, I sat in my hotel room, exhausted and happy, watching myself on television. Once again I was turning the dial and seeing myself being interviewed on every channel— only this time I was a successful businesswoman, not an actress. I couldn't sleep I was so excited. There was no turning back. I knew I was on the right track, and my new career would never disappoint me.

After the Chicago opening, stores from all over the country wanted to carry my cosmetics, and I wanted to see my products everywhere. Often there simply weren't enough weeks in the year for me to attend all the new openings. There were stores I had to convince, but I refused to take no for an answer. Some buyers told me they didn't know how their white customers would react to seeing a black product in the store. I said, "What difference does it make? You have a black customer in the store, too. If you don't give her a product that pleases her, she'll find it somewhere else." I saw to it that my products were always properly displayed, and I was known to pull my line out of a store when I saw it displayed in the back or tucked into an insignificant corner. I invested a lot of my profits in hiring makeup artists to train the black woman, often new to cosmetics, how to apply them properly. Soon I expanded my line to include products for white women as well, to the delight of my mother, who said, "Beauty knows no color barriers. That's the Walden way."

WHAT I'M DOING TODAY

Barbara Walden cosmetics are now found all over the globe. We are constantly expanding and developing our line of products, and I still travel frequently, opening the line in new cities, and helping women of all races and nationalities recognize and enhance their special beauty. I appear regularly on television and radio shows, and visit old-age homes, schools, drug rehabilitation centers, prisons, and job-training programs to teach women of all ages how to put their best face forward in life. Occasionally I accept a small part in a television special or a movie, because some small part of me can never totally renounce my acting career.

BEAUTY IS IMPORTANT TO US

Beauty is especially important to today's black woman. When a woman feels beautiful she also feels confident; her eyes shine, she talks articulately, and she takes important chances. A woman who feels beautiful goes after what she wants—whether it's a job, romance, or changes in her life. Now, more than ever before, black women are ready to pursue important goals, and I want to make sure we have the confidence we need to achieve them.

Women who deny that appearance is important only reveal inhibiting insecurities. Those insecurities change magically to self-confidence when a woman spends the time and effort to achieve the look she wants. I've seen this happen over and over. When I offer to apply makeup on women at my cosmetic counter, I've heard some say, "Don't put your hands on me! I don't care what I look like. You can't do anything with me." Then I persuade that lady to sit on the stool and set to work. Fifteen minutes later I hand her a mirror, hear her ask, "Are you sure this is me?" and see the pleased new expression on her more beautiful face, which I know means the beginning of good things in her life.

WHY YOU SHOULD LOVE YOURSELF

I love myself and am very concerned about myself. I just love being Barbara! Some people might call that selfish vanity, but I call it essential self-love. Vanity, I believe, is a totally positive emotion. Every woman should be vain enough to do the most for the self she loves. If you don't love yourself, how can you ask other people to love you? If you neglect yourself, other people will take the cue and neglect you, too. When I sit across the table from someone, I know I do not see my hair, my clothes, or my face—but that other person does. You can have the greatest mind and soul in the world, but for better or worse, people see the outside first. Taking care of that outside self—investing the time and effort to beautify your skin, perfect your figure, select the right cosmetics and learn to apply them, and choose clothes that become you—shows love not only for yourself, but for the person across the table from you—your employer, your husband or lover, your children, your friends.

INVESTING IN GLAMOUR

Today's glamorous look asks you to invest time, care, and consideration in your beauty. Money is only a small portion of that investment. A shade of lipstick or eyeshadow that's perfect for you is the only one you have to have. One terrific outfit per season, planned to combine with clothes you already own, is all you need. With the right information and practice you can easily care for your skin and hair at home. A lot of my neighbors in Brentwood walk around in the latest fashions, draped with a quarter of a million dollars' worth of jewelry, and they don't look glamorous; they look like Christmas trees! Another wealthy lady I know, always dressed in the latest fashions, walks like a horse; nobody ever bothered to tell her that the most elegant clothes are ugly if you don't carry them well. You can buy a million-dollar dress and have a million-dollar hairdo, but if they are wrong for you, you will have wasted your money and time.

How do you know what is right for you? The answer isn't easy. Real glamour asks you to identify yourself. Open your eyes in front of the mirror and take an objective look at what you've got. Define what's right and what needs improvement. Ask yourself what clothes, hairstyle, and makeup express the image you want to create. Ask yourself if the image you have in mind is really feasible, if it's really you. Don't settle for past images only because they're comfortable, or try for impossible ones. A glamorous woman matches what she has, inside and outside, with the cosmetics, clothes, hairstyling, and skin-beautifying techniques available to her. When the match is perfect, she has style. We black women have always had it.

A glamorous style is a reflection of your individual personality and taste. It can't be copied or created for you by someone else. Style involves a total consciousness of the way your person and surroundings appear to others. To have style, you must also ask yourself what you like—often a surprisingly difficult question to answer. Once I hired a well-known decorator to do my home for me. He created an all-white bedroom, perfectly chic but uncomfortable for me. I complained to a friend of mine who introduced me to the many thrift shops in Los Angeles. In them I bought some old and antique furniture, refinished it to my taste, and soon had a yellow-and-white bedroom—a beautiful room that expressed *me,* not the decorator. Since then I always make sure everything I do for myself involves me.

In order to get what you want in all areas of life, you must first ask yourself, "What do I want? Why?" and "How am I going to get it?" That goes for beauty, too. Before you style your hair a new way, buy a new dress or a new cosmetic, ask yourself, "Do I like this? Is this me? Is this me *now?*" Never simply grab what works for someone else, what you see displayed in an expensive store, or what is shown in a magazine without asking yourself these important questions. This is how unique taste, which expresses your personality and pleases others, is formed.

Before you achieve a sure sense of style and learn how to produce it, you will have to throw away a lot of misconceptions, and invest time and effort in creating the image you have in mind for yourself. Be prepared to make mistakes. Be prepared to get angry and fed up. Be prepared to stop and start over again. Twenty pounds were not gained in a day, and they aren't lost in a day either. Ridding your skin of troublesome blemishes takes consistent care. Choosing the right outfit, hairstyle, and cosmetics requires careful thought and consideration. If you love yourself, you will be prepared to invest in yourself because you know a more beautiful YOU can accomplish beautiful things.

TAKE BARBARA WALDEN TO YOUR DRESSING TABLE

When I was a little girl I used to round up all the children in my neighborhood, take them to my house, bathe them, wash and iron their clothes, fix their hair, and send them back outside looking more beautiful than ever. They didn't always enjoy this game, but I did. I used to comb my mother's long black hair until her head hurt. It was no surprise to her when I started my own cosmetics firm. As an adult I still have a strong desire to make people more beautiful, which is why I have written this book.

In this book I hope to share the valuable techniques and beauty information I have learned from years of working with women across the country. With this book you take *me* into your home—my ideas about skin care, makeup application, hair care and styling; practical information on wardrobe, diet, and exercise; manicuring and pedicuring techniques; and, finally, some special tips to help you put the finishing touches on your glamorous, Star Quality style. I will tell you how to look beautiful by day and beautiful by night. I will tell you how to look beautiful whatever your age. I have also included special beauty information from our dark-skinned sisters in other countries, our "Heritage Secrets." Today we know we are among the world's beautiful women, and I want our beauty, and with it our accomplishments, to be visible to the world.

—*Barbara Walden*

1

Glamour-Right Skin Care

BLACK SKIN IS BEAUTIFUL

We have beautiful skin! Our unique heritage has gifted us with special hidden undertones of orange, yellow, even blue, which project onto the skin's surface to create an incredible variety of colors. Put ten of us in a room and you'll see a flower garden of faces—a subtle range of glowing complexions from pale golden brown to the deepest midnight hue like gorgeous, smooth, black velvet. The same rich pigment that provides our skin with these dramatic inner lights also protects it from the aging ultraviolet rays of the sun and keeps it younger-looking longer.

SKIN CARE COMES FIRST

The face you have now is the only one you're ever going to get! Skin treatment should be the number one priority of your beauty plan. If you spend less than thirty minutes a day cleansing and caring for your skin, you're neglecting the largest, most visible, and, I hope, the prettiest organ in your body. Your skin does not have to look worse as you grow older. Mine looks better now in my forties than it ever has before, because I've learned to control the oils that plagued it through my twenties and to bring out its natural texture and sheen. Little wrinkles and strong character lines can be beautiful on a soft, smooth, mature complexion.

Cosmetics look only as good as the skin you put them on. I always tell my makeup artists to sweep the eye pencils and lipsticks off the counter when they can't convince a customer with troubled skin she needs treatment products more. I do this for selfish reasons. If a customer wears my makeup on skin that's crying for care, she won't help my business. Those carefully designed cosmetics will look all wrong on her unhappy complexion.

You should always cleanse and moisturize the surface of your skin thoroughly *before* you apply makeup for the same reasons you'd spackle a wall, fill in the cracks, and smooth the bumps before giving it a new coat of paint. Never use makeup to camouflage any skin problem that tender loving care and faithful treatment will improve; the cosmetics may cover your problem for the moment, but when you take them off, that depressing naked skin will still be there, staring back at you in the mirror.

TYPECASTING YOUR SKIN

Typecasting your skin is the first step to giving it the glamour-right care it needs to reveal its beauty. Take the following quiz to determine your skin's basic character:

1. Is your skin flaky? Does it show tiny, fine lines? Does it have a rough, sometimes leathery texture? Does it feel like it's shrunk a size after you wash it? Is it sensitive to wind, sunburn, soaps, and steam heating? If so, you are a dry-skin victim.

2. Does your skin often look slick and shiny? Does it have a greasy film, especially in the nose-forehead-chin area, which breaks through makeup? Is it prone to blackheads, whiteheads, pimples, and enlarged pores? If you blot your face with a single sheet of tissue in the morning, does the tissue come away coated with a transparent film? Yes? Your skin is oily—that is, it has bigger glands beneath the surface which produce more oil.

Myths and Fairy Tales

Have you heard that we have oilier skin than white people? Chalk it up to fable. Though our skin *may be* somewhat oilier than the thin, closely pored skin of Celtic types, in general it is no oilier than most people's. Oil on a dark surface, however, reflects light differently than oil on a light surface does; so on us, less *looks* like more. Sorry, it is also a myth that people with oily skin get fewer wrinkles.

3. Is your skin tight and flaky in some areas and slick and shiny in others? You have a common double-jeopardy complexion called "combination skin."

4. Is your skin fresh and moist in appearance, seldom flaky or oily, with a natural matte finish? You are one of the rare beauties with normal skin. Warning: It won't stay that way without the right care.

Remember, your skin often changes its role. Skin always grows drier with age and in response to artificial heating. Oily skins may spout geysers in hot, humid weather, and dry up like depleted wells in the cold. Don't take your skin type for granted; the skin you had as a teenager may now be part of the long-forgotten past and need a different treatment plan. Keep your eyes open and watch for changes.

BARBARA'S BASIC TWO-STEP: THE ALL-SKIN-TYPE CLEANSING PROGRAM

In my years in the cosmetic and skin treatment business, I have found that my personal cleansing program works best for all skin types—with minor modifications for oily and dry skin. Your skin must be cleaned carefully in the morning to rid it of the impurities it has expelled while you sleep. The face must also be thoroughly cleaned before bedtime to remove makeup pigments, bacteria, and air pollutants which have been collected during the day.

Never-Never Number One

Never go to bed with makeup on your face. That's a terrible trick to play on your skin! Though foundation protects your skin from harmful irritants in the atmosphere during the day, it will clog your pores at night, preventing your skin from breathing, resting, and throwing off oils and wastes from its inner layer.

Step 1 If you are wearing makeup, remove it with a commercial cleansing cream. Use a cotton ball and small circular movements, which massage and stimulate circulation in the skin. The oil in the cleansing cream is necessary to dissolve and loosen the pigments in the makeup. A special eye-makeup remover should be used to remove cosmetics that cling tenaciously to the sensitive tissue around the eyes. Remove all traces of cleanser with cotton balls.

Never-Never Number Two

Soap is a fine cleanser for dirty clothes and floors, but keep this harsh stuff off your face. Even the mildest soaps are drying (especially for already dry or delicate skins) and leave a hard-to-remove residue. Women with oily skin often tell me they don't feel "clean" unless they wash their faces with soap; they believe soap cuts down the extra oils. Soap, in my opinion, only dries the fragile surface of the skin without drying the ever-active oil glands beneath, which keep on spouting the oil. In fact, if you overwash (i.e., overdry) the surface of your skin with soap, you can actually signal the oil glands to overcompensate in order to replace the missing oils. I use soap on my hands and private areas and banish it from the rest of my body. A bath with soap turns me into a total flake!

Water-soluble cleansing lotions may be less irritating than your trusty bar, but they still contain soap or soaplike substances. Often the directions do not specify "remove with water." Any soap or lotion left on the skin will cause dryness, and cellular buildup, and will eventually damage your skin permanently, making it sensitive and dull. Neither soap nor lotion have the pigment-cutting action necessary to lift makeup from the face. If you don't believe me and *must* use a soap or soap-based cleanser, be sure to wash it off thoroughly with fifteen splashes of tepid water. If you have dry skin, throw your soap away.

CLEANSING CREAMS FROM YOUR KITCHEN

If you don't want to buy a commercial cleansing cream, you can find excellent equivalents in your kitchen. Try mayonnaise—a rich, proteinized oily cleanser—baby oil, unscented castor oil, any vegetable oil, or plain Vaseline petroleum jelly. These are a bit messier than commercial products, but they work.

The main ingredient in commercial eye-makeup-remover pads is mineral oil. Make your own dollarwise version by cutting gauze pads into squares, stacking them in a clean, empty cleansing cream jar, and drenching them with baby oil or plain mineral oil until the pads are thoroughly soaked.

HERITAGE SECRETS

Cleopatra's Cleanser

Egyptians believed that walnut oil stymied the growth of facial hair. This may be an ancient myth, but walnut oil *does* make an excellent makeup-removing cleanser. Apply it with a cotton ball and use as you would a commercial cleansing cream. Walnut oil, available in health-food stores or specialty-food stores, is also a highly nutritious salad oil.

Step 2 After you're removed your makeup, wash away all remaining residues of dirt, cosmetics, and cleanser with a freshener. If you weren't wearing makeup to begin with, use the freshener alone—it will take care of bacteria, oils, and pollutants without the help of soap or water. Soak cotton balls or pads with the freshener, then stroke with upward, sweeping motions over your face. When the pad comes away clean, your face is clean, too. The freshener will not only cleanse but help close pores and smooth the surface of the skin by removing the dead skin cells which dim your complexion.

Most fresheners contain small quantities of alcohol (unlike astringents, which are alcohol-based), other mild cleansers, and sometimes moisturizing agents. Try different brands until you find the one that works best with your skin type.

Kitchen Freshener

My grandmother taught me her secret formula for a simple-to-make freshener that works magic on darker skins. Simply squeeze the juice of one lemon into a quart of water, and store this lemon freshener in the refrigerator in a glass jar. Lemon has a good oil-cutting property and in undiluted form can remove stains on the skin. This mild, icy lemon freshener is an excellent clarifying agent for our dark complexions. It complements the skin's own acid balance and gives it a fresh, radiant tone. If your skin tingles unpleasantly when you use the lemon freshener, squeeze only the juice of half a lemon into the quart of water.

Rubbing half a lemon on knees and elbows clouded with dark areas of pigment on a daily basis will help remove these "melanin stains." A drop of pure lemon juice applied to a pimple with a Q-Tip cotton swab will help dry it, too.

Never-Never Number Three

Never use tissues to apply treatment products to your skin. The tissues will absorb the substance and therefore put less of it on your face. They are also made of woody fibers, which are rough on the skin.

Never-Never Number Four

Banish harsh abrasive cleansers from your face unless they have been specifically prescribed by a dermatologist. The polyester-fiber sponge, a scratchy little monster, and other harsh grains and scrubs remove the cells from the *stratum corneum* (in plain English, top layer). These cells belong where they are; they protect the inner layer of the skin from brutal enemies in the atmosphere. The "dead" cells composing the top layer of skin get washed away in due time via normal cleansing. For an extra cell-removing boost (often beneficial for the mature skin, which doesn't shed its excess cells as rapidly), try the mildly abrasive but natural Egyptian Almond Scrub, the cornmeal and buttermilk scrub in the Smoothie Ash-Banishing Facial (see page 36), or the Bran and Yogurt Masque (see page 22).

Every night of my life I sleep on a clean towel placed over my pillowcase. The gentle friction of my cheek turning on the terrycloth towel helps stimulate circulation in my face and loosens dead skin cells and impurities.

HERITAGE SECRETS

Egyptian Almond Scrub

Dusky-skinned Egyptian women were the first to discover the skin-cleansing and softening properties of almonds, an ingredient in many modern scrubs. Make your own Egyptian almond cleanser by grinding unblanched almonds finely in your electric blender. You can also purchase already ground almonds in the form of almond meal in some health-food stores. Wet your face and place about two tablespoons of the ground almonds in your palm. Add enough milk (as the Egyptians did) or water to make a grainy paste and massage it into your skin. The almonds provide a natural abrasive that helps loosen blackheads and remove dead skin cells. They also release a milky substance that does wonders for softening skin. You can add a half teaspoon of honey to the same almond paste to help close and tighten pores. Rinse thoroughly.

ONCE-A-WEEK DEEP-CLEANSING FACIAL

Everyone on earth owes themselves a deep-cleansing facial once a week. This essential facial gets deep down into the skin to pull out superficial blackheads, plus other grit and grime; it temporarily tightens pores and lets moisture accumulate in the skin, giving it a smooth, refreshed appearance.

To deep-cleanse, you need a masque. For oily, normal, and combination skins, a clay-based or mint-type commercial masque cleans most effectively. If your skin is dry, try beating a few drops of olive oil into the commercial product. Gel-based or "peel-off" masques will tighten pores but do not have the dirt-loosening power of clay-based masques.

Your once-a-week facial should follow your regular makeup-removing cleanser. Spread the commercial or homemade product on your skin, close your eyes, and relax for twenty minutes. Rinse off the masque with cold water to tighten pores and wake up the skin. Use a clean washcloth to help. Follow with your cleansing freshener to remove any remaining traces of the masque. Don't overdo: A once-a-week masque is enough. If you deep-cleanse more often, the process will be ineffective and possibly irritating.

Easy Kitchen Masques

1. Grandmother's Egg-on-the-Face Masque

My grandmother beat an entire egg and patted the yellow icky mess on her face once a week. We children thought she was crazy, but grandma was crazy like a fox: Her skin remained lovely her entire life. The protein in the egg nourishes the skin, and the white tightens the pores. Beat in a teaspoon of honey for an additional pore-tightening, softening ingredient.

2. Avocado Smash Masque

Avocados have long been used in cosmetic preparations for their rich oils, vitamins, and cleansing properties. I pluck one from a tree in my backyard, mash a quarter of the avocado (or half of a small one), beat it with one egg yolk and two teaspoons of orange juice, and pat it lightly on my face. If you don't have time to mix up the preceding recipe, a few tablespoons of avocado alone, finely mashed, will suffice.

3. Bran and Yogurt Masque

Mix one tablespoon of raw bran (available in supermarkets and health-food stores) with two tablespoons of plain yogurt and one teaspoon of wheat germ or vegetable oil. Mix to form a thick paste and apply with your fingertips, using gentle, circular motions. The bran helps slough off dead skin cells, the yogurt cleanses, cools, and tightens, and the rich oil lubricates.

HERITAGE SECRETS

West African Pumpkin-seed Facial

Here is my version of a very special masque from West Africa that you can make at home. Place one tablespoon of pumpkin seeds, half a cucumber, half a cup of milk, and two or three drops of lemon juice in a blender. (In Africa they grind this mixture together by hand.) Blend for five minutes and apply to your face. Leave it on for fifteen minutes and rinse off with tepid water.

Triple Oil Control

If your skin is oilier than the Persian Gulf, you can control the excess by adding another step to your basic cleansing program. Three times a week, after you have removed your makeup with cleanser, wipe an astringent (containing a large percentage of alcohol) onto the oily areas of your face with a cotton pad until the pad comes away clean. Remove as much of the oily cleanser as you can with the cotton first. If your entire face is oily, this astringent will replace the milder freshener you use the rest of the week. If you have combination skin, use the astringent on the oily areas, and cleanse the normal and dry areas with freshener. If you are not wearing makeup, simply use your astringent as described above.

HERITAGE SECRETS

Barbados Daiquiri Astringent

This special astringent comes from a very good friend who was born and raised in Barbados. She uses it to cleanse and clarify her oily skin. Mix one ounce of white rum with two ounces of rose water or orange water (available in spice stores and specialty-food stores), and apply to your skin with cotton balls. This special skin cocktail leaves the skin extremely soft and helps reduce enlarged pores. It's not for the dry-skin victim, however.

Kitchen Astringents

Slice a raw potato and press the slices onto your oily areas. The potato contains an astringent property that will absorb extra oils. Tomato slices, too, can be used as an astringent (but not on acned skin). A solution of half rubbing alcohol and half water makes a crude but drying astringent. Plain alcohol, I feel, is just too drying for anyone.

Oil-blotting Facial

Once a week squeeze an orange and soak cotton pads in the juice. Lie down and apply the pads to the oily areas of your face for twenty minutes. The orange juice will neutralize extra oils, and smooth and tighten skin.

Moisturize, Moisturize!

Every skin cries out for moisturizer. This precious skin restorer does not actually add moisture, but provides an invisible barrier that prevents water, your skin's natural moisturizing agent, from evaporating. Moisturizer makes skin smoother and softer; it allows makeup to slide on easily, softens tiny lines and wrinkles, and improves the overall texture. Even oily skins need a moisturizer, because the moisture it preserves (H_2O) is not the same as oil. A light moisturizer containing *water* (look for it on the label) will blend best with the surface of your skin. Don't forget to apply it to the area around your eyes, which lacks oil glands and dries out easily. Always apply moisturizer after cleansing.

Dry-skin Victims

Don't make a move without your moisturizer! When you are not wearing makeup, apply it and reapply it. Carry a small bottle in your purse. You can even dab extra moisturizer on superdry areas over makeup. You always need special protection against the drying effects of indoor heating, sun, and wind.

Myths and Fairy Tales

Heavy night creams do not, I repeat, do *not* remove wrinkles and may actually help to age your skin because they clog pores and prevent it from breathing naturally while you sleep. Exotic ingredients (mink, shark, turtle oils) only jack up the price of these mythical youth creams and do nothing to take your wrinkles away or to prevent them from forming. (See "wrinkles" under "Troubleshooting" (page 30) for the truth about wrinkles.) Your regular sheer moisturizer makes a good lubricating night cream.

The Miracle Skin Rejuvenator

Researchers have recently discovered that one of the most fabulous ingredients for keeping your skin young and soft comes in that ordinary glass jar you've had sitting on your dressing table for years—Vaseline petroleum jelly! As you get older your skin does not shed its top layer of cells as rapidly as it did when you were young. The result: a buildup of old cells which tends to make your skin look rough and coarse. Believe it or not, the ingredients in plain old petroleum jelly really help the skin shed its old cells and keep you looking younger. Try substituting a light touch of Vaseline for your regular night cream or moisturizer while you sleep.

HERITAGE SECRETS

Egyptian Bread Masque

Papyrus sheets, found in ancient Egyptian tombs, record this beauty-conscious culture's elaborate recipes for skin treatments. One, a special concoction of flour and milk, kept Egyptian ladies' skin soft. The next time you are making a yeast bread, save a cup of the risen dough for your face. Spread it on your skin as you would any masque and let it firm and tighten for twenty minutes. Remove with water and a washcloth. This Egyptian masque is especially good for the mature complexion.

GLAMOROUS SKIN: THE INSIDE STORY

There's more to your skin than meets the eye. This attractive body wrapper is actually a double-layered organ; the condition of the layer you don't see, below the surface, plays a mighty role in determining how the outer layer appears to the world. The outside of your skin is composed of living cells, coated with a protective barrier of dead cells which are gradually shed or pushed aside by the new cells. We help these dead cells fall away by cleansing our faces and keeping them full and plump by moisturizing. Pigment, which gives our skin its deep, special tones, is also located on the outer layer. Just below the surface lie lubricating (sometimes infuriating) oil glands, ending on the surface in small holes called pores. The invisible inner layer is the home of sweat glands, hair roots, and the all-important blood vessels, which transport nourishment and moisturizing water to the greedy cells outside. The inner layer also provides support for the skin with bundles of tough, elastic tissues; these tissues determine the smoothness and resiliency of your skin and tend to deteriorate with age. Damage to the supporting tissues in the form of deep cuts, scarring skin diseases, or serious and long-term sunburn, will result in permanent damage to the outside layer. If you want beautiful skin, then, you must give the life-support systems on the inside layer attention and care. Here's how:

1. REACH FOR WATER instead of something else. Water is the main moisturizing ingredient of the skin and is fed to the surface via the blood vessels. The more water you drink the greater the supply available to your skin, which is often parched by weather conditions and indoor heating. By water I do not mean juices, soda, coffee, tea, or alcohol: I mean *pure, fresh 100 percent water*. Experts recommend eight glasses a day, but if eight ounces times eight makes you feel like a rubber raft, try drinking six, or even four. I begin each morning with a glass of this wholesome, refreshing, nonfattening elixir and keep one by my bed at night. Reserve a jar of cold water in the refrigerator and go for it when you're thirsty. If the tap water in your area tastes like chemical waste, make a gallon of spring water part of your grocery list. Whenever you're in a restaurant, drink water (down the first glass and order a second—it's free!) instead of other beverages. When you have a cup of coffee, drink a glass of water, too. An excellent before-dinner cocktail is a glass of sparkling water with a twist of lemon. Water will not only improve the texture of your skin but flush toxins, which cause blemishes, out of your system and assist your bladder and intestinal functions as well.

2. AVOID CONSTIPATION, a serious skin clouder and blemish maker. Chronic constipation allows toxic wastes to seep out of the intestinal tract and back into your system—a problem that lowers your resistance to infection and causes bad breath as well as skin problems. Don't take the easy way out with over-the-counter laxatives, which ultimately make your body too lazy to do the job itself and the problem worse. (Keep milk of magnesia on the

outside; it makes an excellent cleansing masque for the face!) Get
into natural laxatives: Add bran to yogurt, packaged cereals, and
baked goods; eat raw carrots, fruits, and lightly cooked fresh
vegetables. Another tip: Never postpone that important urge.

3. START HUFFIN' AND PUFFIN'. An aerobic exercise (running, swimming, rope jumping, modern dance, tennis, squash, or paddleball) will benefit your entire body. You may be surprised to learn these thigh-trimming, waist-slimming, healthy heart-beaters also improve your skin by sending more blood at greater speed to the tiny blood vessels beneath the surface, nourishing them with an increased supply of food and water. Aerobic exercise also detoxifies the skin by flushing out blemish-causing wastes faster. The end result: a deep, glowing light from within.

4. STOP INDULGING. Bad habits can be fun but they have a definite negative effect on the skin. Huffin' and puffin' should not include smoking—one of the worst things you can do for your complexion. Smoking cuts off circulation to the skin, causing premature wrinkling, especially around the eyes and mouth, which you purse up to do the "puffin'"! Ladies who smoke always end up with rough, dry skin at the prime of life.

Excess caffeine (coffee, tea, colas) will also roughen your skin. Cut down on this toxic substance for a smoother, brighter complexion. Try substituting herbal teas, juices, and water for these nerve-jangling skin destroyers.

Drugs and alcohol in excess will also damage your skin along with the rest of your body.

A good "bad habit" for your skin is called "love." Make as much of it as possible. Your face will reflect your inner glow.

5. DREAM SWEETLY. Good times often go with late hours. Though fun can be a wonderful pick-me-up for a blah skin, don't overdo. Remember, rest and sleep are essential to a pretty complexion, especially as the years pile on. A tired face is usually a haggard one, and dark circles and character lines grow more pronounced with exhaustion. If you suffer from insomnia, try to relax with a gentle stretching exercise like yoga (but not just before bedtime). Substitute calcium supplements for harmful sleeping pills.

6. FEED YOUR SKIN. Skin is hungry and needs proper nourishment to reach its most healthy state. A junk-food diet will never do.

Proteins are essential to make new tissues and skin cells. If you don't eat enough in the form of meat, fish, dairy products, peas, and beans, the body will raid its own tissues for the protein it craves. When tissues in the skin's elastic foundation give up important cells, the foundation caves in and wrinkles and grooves result.

Vitamin A is also an important skin food; lack of it can stop oil in the pores from reaching the surface, creating a sandpaper complexion. Fish liver oils, carrots (my favorite), and raw or lightly cooked dark-green vegetables supply the A you need. Don't OD on Vitamin A supplements; too much of this good thing can be toxic.

Vitamin A Tonic Toner: If you have an electric vegetable juicer, combine ten ounces of carrot juice with six ounces of spinach juice for a vitamin-packed, natural skin-clearing tonic.

The B vitamins help reduce stress, which aggravates skin problems. The best sources of Vitamin B are liver and brewers' yeast. Brewers' yeast is a yellow, flour-like substance which can be mixed into juices, sprinkled on salads, or added to baked goods. Try the tasty, bright-yellow, "farm-grown" variety available in health-food stores. Liver and yeast are both a source of Vitamin B_2, an excess-oil controller. Folic acid, also present in liver, helps clear skin of dark blotches.

All vegetable oils, except olive and peanut oil, supply low cholesterol fatty acids, important for preventing dry skin and skin diseases like eczema and psoriasis.

HERITAGE SECRETS

Exotic Asian Facial

An important food staple in China and Japan is called *tofu,* or bean curd. This low-calorie, protein- and vitamin-packed, white cheese-like food (available in health-food stores and Asian food shops) makes a nourishing facial masque. Put half a block of bean curd in your blender with a quarter cup of milk and blend until smooth. Apply thickly to your face and leave for twenty minutes. Presto! The smooth, closely pored skin our Asian sisters are famous for is yours!

Dry-skin Victims: If your skin is exceptionally dry all the time, try adding two tablespoons of corn or safflower oil to your daily diet.

7. CHECK THE PILLS AND MEDICATIONS YOU ARE TAKING. If you develop dark patches, unusual rashes, or sudden breakouts, take a look into your medicine chest: The culprit may live there. Birth control pills, in combination with sunlight, can produce dark splotches known as *chloasma.* Other medications produce the same condition along with rashes or hives. The bromides in many medicines can aggravate acne. New cosmetics, too, may cause allergies and skin flareups. Many people are allergic to so-called "natural" ingredients and perfumes in cosmetic products.

8. COOL SUN EXPOSURE. Have you heard that black people don't burn? Nonsense: We *do* burn; *I* burn; many of my customers tell me *they* burn. And I can vouch for what happens to Sammy Davis, Jr.'s father when he goes fishing. The sun really burns his skin. Though, in general, we can withstand three to five times more sun than light-skinned people, we do suffer skin damage as a result of overexposure—especially in southern or tropical climates. Even if you don't burn, sunbaking year after year will age your skin faster than the calendar, making it as tough and wrinkled as a piece of old leather, and will magnify the dark spots that tend to come with age. Overdoses of sun also break down the tissues beneath the skin, creating sags and bags.

If you enjoy the sun, give yourself some protection with a sunscreen containing 5 percent PABA to filter out harmful ultraviolet rays. Though we seldom get skin cancer, it *can* happen to ladies with lighter complexions.

Sun Protection from Your Kitchen

The special rich oil that collects inside the skin of an avocado creates an excellent sun-protection moisturizer for the skin. Spread it on and leave it there while sunbathing.

Sesame oil both lubricates the skin and provides a mild sunscreen.

9. DON'T STRETCH AND PULL THE MUSCLES OF YOUR FACE. Facial massages, I believe, will stretch your skin unless done occasionally by trained professionals. Another way to stretch your

skin, implanting sags and wrinkles, is to pull at your face with your hands or rest your cheek in your palm. Many of us have these bad habits. Though many people may tell you differently, I believe that facial exercises are also aging to the skin. When you do facial exercises, the muscles beneath your skin expand, plumping it out on top; but as they expand, they also stretch the skin. If you follow a strict regimen of facial exercises and absolutely never take vacations, you *may* help your skin stay taut and youthful. If you do the exercises for several years, however, then stop, or do them inconsistently, the muscles you've expanded will deflate, leaving you with only the stretched and sagging skin. The best way to keep your face smooth, slim, and youthful is to practice a regular aerobic exercise, which burns extra fat off your entire body, including your face.

TROUBLESHOOTING

Many troubles plague our skin, some small and easily resolved, others serious and maddeningly resistant to care. Whatever your problem, don't give up; where there's life, there's hope! The sciences of dermatology and cosmetology are now at their most advanced stage in history, and new discoveries are being made all the time. Below is a rundown of the most common skin problems and the best-known ways to attack them.

Problem: Acne Blues

Acne is an inflammatory disease of the oil glands in the skin. The sick little glands produce too much oil and the cells that line them stick together, preventing the oil from reaching the surface and floating harmlessly away. The trapped oil forms an invisible plug below the surface. Bacteria attack the plug, causing it to grow and break through the walls of the duct and inflame the surrounding tissues. The end product is your unfriendly pimple, or cyst. Blackheads are just a minor form of acne—the same plug of oil, bacteria, and cells, pushed up to the surface of the skin where it is oxidized by the air and turns dark.

Acne is thought to be caused by an excess of male hormone, or androgen (present in women, too), and/or a special sensitivity to it. The breakout blues commonly strike during adolescence, when the body's hormones are aroused and changing, but often afflict women in their late twenties and early thirties, too. A few unlucky souls bear this adolescent cross through menopause. Acne may flare up around your menstrual period (when hormones are active), when you stop or start taking birth control pills, in response to stress, or to a change in the environment or certain foods. Sorry, we are just as prone to acne as our light-skinned sisters, though a *mild* case may not look as obvious on our darker skins. The term "acne" describes not only the inflamed bumps and pits syndrome, but a persistent crop of pimples and black-heads as well.

The Cure

Good news! Acne can be controlled, if not always totally cured, with the help of a dermatologist. Whenever a lady with a serious acne problem arrives at my counter, I immediately refer her to a doctor because I know there are new ways to treat this condition that did not exist even ten years ago. Dermatologists make war on acne with a variety of antibiotics, taken internally or applied to the skin in a topical solution—a drying medication called benzoyl peroxide—as well as other effective treatments. Acne cysts are injected with a steroid, blackheads removed, and home-cleansing treatments prescribed.

If you have acne, it is important to get professional help as soon as possible before scarring occurs. Scarring creates special problems for black skin because the scars themselves are difficult to treat. Dermabrasion, a corrective process in which the skin is literally sanded to remove scars, is not advisable for our skin because it is bound to leave pigment irregularities or even larger scars. For similar reasons we should *not* attempt to cure our own acne with over-the-counter medications. Benzoyl peroxide, avail-able in drugstores, may not be a suitable treatment for many black skins because it can produce dark blotches. Leave it to the pros! If you can't afford a private doctor, most hospitals have excellent dermatology clinics. It's better to pay with dollars now than with tears later.

Choosing the Right Dermatologist

Black skin responds to the new acne treatments a bit differently than white skin, because the top layer is a little thicker, making it harder for some medications to penetrate. A well-trained dermatologist will be able to account for this difference when he prescribes medication. A white dermatologist is just as capable of treating black skin as a black dermatologist. All modern dermatology training includes the black skin and its problems, and this subject is part of every dermatologist's residency and an oft-discussed subject at professional meetings.

Never-Never Number Five

Never, never attack a pimple with your fingernails. No one should pick and squeeze, but we *must* not because of our susceptibility to hyperpigmentation (see page 33) and difficult-to-treat scars. If you can't resist a blackhead, use a metal blackhead extractor (clean it with alcohol first), or press, ever so gently, with your fingers wrapped in tissue. If the blemish isn't squeezable, leave it alone!

Home Remedy for Acne

The best thing you can do for acne at home is to soak a clean washcloth in very hot water, fold it into a compress, and press it to the infected area. Hot compresses do wonders for soft-tissue infections like acne because they mobilize blood to the area, which helps the skin fight the infection and bring it to a head. I also recommend keeping makeup off the infected area until the problem is under control. To help dry an occasional pimple, cover it with your clay-based masque and leave it on overnight.

Diet and Acne: Barbara Speaks Out!

Dermatologists claim that what you eat does not affect acne and say they have performed tests which prove that no amount of chocolate, peanuts, colas, and other junk have the slightest effect on blemish-prone skin. When the dermatologists have performed this test on every single person in the world, then I will believe them and only then. In the meantime, I can only speak for

Barbara! I know for a fact that when I eat chocolate or bacon (my all-time favorite food) or anything fried, my skin breaks out. Recently I was a guest on a TV talk show with one of New York's leading skin doctors. He declared that anyone with acne can eat candy and french fries without making the condition worse. I said to myself, "I hope that man is right because I would *love* to be able to eat french fries." When I got back to Los Angeles, I went straight into the kitchen and made the big, thick fries I adore. The next morning there my problem was again! That dermatologist might be right about every other person, but he was wrong about Barbara! I've always had a tendency toward blemishes, and certain foods bring them out—no ifs, ands or buts about it.

Everybody's internal workings are different and everyone's skin, I firmly believe, is affected by different foods. If you are a longtime acne victim, I recommend giving up sugar (and everything with sugar in it), fried foods, white breads and refined flours, and fatty meats like beef and pork. Substitute fish and poultry, fresh fruits and vegetables, and whole wheat breads and grains. This may be worse than death for some junk-food fans, but give it a try. At least drastically cut your consumption of the no-no's for three months. (It will take that long to get the unhealthy residues out of your system.) Make lists of everything you eat in a day and try to tally the foods on those lists with recurrent flareups. Three months later if your skin is as bad as ever, go back to your diet of sweets and junk with the famous doctor's blessing. Giving the stuff up for a while, however, will never hurt you; you'll certainly slim down and feel better, and Barbara Walden will bet your skin will improve.

Never-Never Number Six

If you have acne, avoid kelp and seaweed, and stay away from large quantities of seafood. Dermatologists are sure that the iodides in these foods aggravate the skin.

Problem: Post-inflammatory Hyperpigmentation (or PIHP)

PIHP is a problem that besets all skin, black and white, but we are more susceptible because we have extra pigment to begin with.

When the skin becomes inflamed, melanocytes, or pigment-producing cells, may get disturbed, produce more pigment, and disperse it. The result: a dark area surrounding the site of an acne flareup, psoriasis, or other rashes, that remains long after the inflammatory condition has died down. Those areas of dark pigment may occur any place on the body.

The Cure

Again, head for your dermatologist. This problem is serious! First, you must cure the inflammatory condition that's producing the pigmentation. The scarring, too, will not fade easily without professional treatment. A dermatologist has various methods to eliminate the excess pigment, including individually tailored bleaching creams which may include cortisone and a preparation to induce superficial peeling. Dermatologists do not recommend over-the-counter bleaching creams; they are either weak and completely ineffective or can overshoot the mark, making the bleached area *lighter* than the surrounding skin. Even low-strength bleaching creams may cause an overreaction in some folks, or create allergic reactions in combination with the sunlight. This tricky cream, whether prescribed or purchased over the counter, must be placed on the *exact spot you want to lighten*—not all over your face or body. If you suffer from hyperpigmentation, you must hide the dark areas from the sun, which will make them darker, or use a protective lotion containing UVA as well as UVB sunscreens to eliminate different lengths of ultraviolet waves.

Never-Never Number Seven

Never put a bleaching cream on your face for any reason without testing it on an invisible area near your hairline for a period of a week or two.

Problem: *Dermatosis Papulosa Nigra*

This is a fancy medical term for tiny dark warts, which may surface by the hundreds on the neck, face, and other parts of the body. All people get these harmless raised spots, but we get them at an earlier age, and we get them darker because more dark pigment is incorporated into them. Women are more prone to have them than men.

The Cure

Papulosa nigra are not necessarily a problem. If you like them you can keep them; but if you find them unattractive, they can be easily and almost painlessly removed with an electric needle or a little round knife by a dermatologist. Often he or she will remove one or two before the others to make sure no white spot will be left behind.

Myths and Fairy Tales

Some people believe these tiny warts cannot be removed, that they are malignant, or that to remove them will cause cancer. All these assumptions are false!

Problem: Keloid Scarring

A keloid is a huge raised scar which can occur at sites of burns, operations, injuries, or even severe acne. The fibrous tissue at the site of trauma goes crazy, and the cells run amok and reproduce at a tremendous rate. The result: a disfiguring scar. Black people are susceptible to keloids, which tend to form on the chest, the upper part of the back, and the earlobe. The face and scalp are less likely to sprout them.

Keloids strike without rhyme or reason. If you've had one keloid, you are keloid-prone, which means you may develop another, or you may not. If you've never had a keloid, you may still suffer one at some time in your life. It is impossible for a doctor to predict who will or will not grow these scars. Keloids, moreover, are by no means rare. For this reason dermatologists believe it is a significant risk for *any* black woman to pierce her ears—a prime location for keloid development. If anyone in your family has had a keloid, or if you've ever had one yourself, *don't* take the chance. Keloids may not develop immediately after a trauma to the skin, but may take weeks, even months, to form.

The Cure

Once you have a keloid there is no happy solution. It can be flattened through a long series of treatments, which include injecting it with steroids or operating on it. The operation itself may produce another monstrous scar, however, though doctors can inject the first keloid with steroids at the time of surgery to avoid this complication. If you develop a keloid on an earlobe, you will never have quite the same lobe you did before—even after months of expensive medical procedures.

Problem: Ashy Skin

Ashy skin is simply extremely dry, flaky skin. White people have "ashes," too, but they aren't as visible on their lighter-colored skins. We are most susceptible to ash in winter, when artificial heating and cold, dry air conspire to parch our complexions.

The Cure

If you have "ashes," you must treat your skin gently. Avoid soap (on both face and body) at all costs and skip very hot baths, showers, steam rooms, and saunas. Make sure you protect your skin with a coat of good, penetrating moisturizer and an oil-based makeup foundation. You may want to use a richer lotion on your body, or Vaseline. Follow the prescriptions for "dehydrated skin" (see below) as well.

Smoothie Ash-banishing Facial

1. Once a week make a paste of two tablespoons of cornmeal (the fine-ground variety) and four tablespoons of buttermilk. Apply it to the skin, massaging in with gentle, circular motions. This will help loosen the "ashes," and the paste can be used on knees and elbows as well as on your face. Leave the paste on for five minutes, remove it with tepid water, and pat (not rub) your skin dry with a towel.

2. Now heat one ounce of olive oil in a pan until it is warm (not hot) and apply it with upward strokes to your face and neck with a cotton ball.

3. Remove the excess olive oil with a clean, moist cotton ball and let what remains soak into your skin. This is a good prebedtime treatment.

Problem: Dehydrated Skin

Dehydrated skin can be oily as well as dry. This thirsty skin looks porous, lacks a supple, smooth texture, is dull and does not shine. Like dry skin, dehydrated skin reveals every wrinkle and line. Dehydration may be the result of an illness which has caused you to lose a lot of fluids, overconsumption of alcohol and coffee, harsh soaps whose residues have piled up on your skin, as well as winter weather conditions or sunbaking.

The Cure

To rehydrate, you must refill your skin's depleted water reservoirs. Begin drinking eight glasses of water a day (no excuses, eight full glasses). Cut down on caffeinated beverages and alcohol. Replace your soap or cleansing-lotion-and-water routine with my two-step program. Needless to say, you must not forget your moisturizer.

It is also important to keep your environment as moist as possible. (The secret of the famous "English" complexion is rainy weather.) Invest in a humidifier for your home, or at least buy a smaller one for your bedroom. Cover radiators with wet towels or place pans of water on top. Keep your heating system as low as possible; you'll save energy while you save your skin. I also recommend filling a plant sprayer with mineral water and spritzing your face with it often.

Two Hydrating Facials

This gentle steam treatment will put moisture back into your skin. Try it once a week.

1. Put two tablespoons of camomile flowers (available in health-food stores) and a tablespoon of dried rosemary into a pot of water. Cover the pot and boil your "herb tea" for five minutes. Remove the top of the pot and place it on a low table. Wearing

sunglasses or goggles to protect your eyes, place your face two feet above the pot and allow the steam to penetrate your thirsty pores for five minutes. Follow with moisturizer.

2. This "compress rehydration treatment" is easier and can be done while you're bathing.

Soak a hand towel in tepid water, or in the cooled, strained "herb tea" described above. Fold towel into a compress and press over your face. Come up for air when necessary, but leave the moist compress in contact with your skin for as long as possible. Seal in the water with moisturizer applied to your still-damp face. This is a good treatment for dry skin, too, and can be done as often as you like.

Warning: If you suffer from dry skin or dehydrated skin, don't use bleaching creams until the condition improves. Bleaching creams contain bismuth or mercury salts, which are very drying.

Problem: Enlarged Pores

What we call a pore is really the end of the tube-shaped oil duct beneath the skin's surface. Oil is excreted through the pores and helps lubricate the surface of the skin and keep it soft. Enlarged pores occur when excess oil gets stuck in the duct, stretching it out. Once the extra fatty acids are removed, the pores can close back up to their normal size. If pores are constantly stretched out of shape, however, they eventually become permanently enlarged. Pores also tend to appear larger as we age.

The Cure

If your skin is oily, you risk a permanent case of enlarged pores. Start controlling excess oils as soon as possible by keeping your face scrupulously clean, using an alcohol-based astringent in oily or large-pored areas, and never skipping your deep-cleansing facial. Two heaping tablespoons of brewers' yeast in tomato or orange juice twice a day will help control oils from within. The following facial encourages pores to release their impurities and gives them a smoother, tighter appearance.

Pore-shrinking Facial

1. Fill a pot with water and add two tablespoons of baking soda. Boil the water for five minutes with the cover on, then remove the cover and make a tent for your face and the pot with a sheet or towel. Protect your eyes with goggles or sunglasses. The steam should be very hot to clean out the pores. Steam your face for fifteen minutes.

2. Beat the white of an egg with a few drops of lemon juice and apply to your face. The egg white is an old-fashioned, effective tightening masque. Leave on for twenty minutes.

3. Remove the masque with steeped, cooled tea. (The tea should be a high-quality bulk type. Inferior teas contain dyes.) The tannin in the tea provides an excellent pore tightener. Follow with moisturizer.

Any one of the three steps of this facial will prove effective. You can use cooled tea as a regular astringent. For a fragrant change, add two tablespoons of spearmint or mint leaves to the water of your "steam bath" in place of baking soda.

HERITAGE SECRETS

North African Henna Masque

North African and Middle Eastern women have long used henna to improve the condition of their hair and skin. To make your own version of a North African henna masque, mix three tablespoons of pure *neutral* henna with three tablespoons of water. Add a tablespoon of plain yogurt and mix into a thick paste. Apply this oil-balancing mixture to your face for ten to fifteen minutes, then rinse off thoroughly.

Problem: Wrinkles

There is no way to avoid death, taxes, and wrinkles. These telltale grooves and lines appear sooner or later when elastic fibers beneath the skin break down and the muscles in the face lose cells. At what point this process occurs depends largely on your hereditary timetable; you will probably find wrinkles on your face about the year your mother or father did. Fortunately, our dark pigment protects our skin from the sun, one of youth's main enemies. Overexposure to this wrinkling villain, however, will speed up the aging process. Crash diets also cause wrinkles. These low-calorie, nutrition-short reducing plans rapidly strip our bodies of fat, and may do the same to our faces, creating pockets, wrinkles, and sags. Lose your extra pounds gradually on a well-rounded diet containing all the vitamins and minerals. Consider that as you get older a bit of extra "face filler" in the form of fat may help you retain a smooth, youthful complexion.

Though wrinkles are inevitable, a "happy" line engraved in your face from years of smiling is more attractive than the nasty lines you get from frowning, squinting, or turning down your mouth to make negative expressions. If you want to work on your wrinkles, work on your peace of mind. Happiness, contentment, self-acceptance, and simple joy are your emotional insurance policy for a pretty older face.

The Cure

Sorry, ladies, there are no bona fide cures for wrinkles as of the twentieth century. No creams, lotions, vitamins, or magic potions will erase these "life-expression" lines once they're engraved. A good diet, rest, healthy habits, and a proper cleansing and moisturizing program can keep your skin soft, radiant, and youthful in texture. Start practicing what I've been preaching. A regular eye checkup and the glasses you may need are good wrinkle preventatives, too, because squinting can plant lines around your eyes.

Problem: Puffy Eyes

Puffy circles under the eyes can be caused by lack of sleep, too much sleep, fluids which accumulate due to faulty digestion or malfunctioning organs, tension, pollution, and allergic reactions to cosmetic products. Sometimes the "puffs" are a hereditary feature, an unwanted gift from one of your parents.

The Cure

If your eyes suddenly grow puffy, itchy, or sore, examine the new soaps, perfumes, or creams on your dressing table—one of them may be the culprit. Many people are allergic to cosmetic substances and/or perfumes. Don't put night creams and moisturizers too close to the eyes—they may get into them, causing eye tissues to swell while you sleep. Avoid eating for four hours before bedtime and sleep with your head on two pillows to help fluids accumulating in the eye tissues drain downward. If your eyes tend to be puffy, never pull or rub the tissue around them with your fingers.

To reduce swelling try the following:

1. Wash out your eyes with cold water or a mild boric acid solution (available at your pharmacy).

2. Apply leftover cooled tea bags to the eye area. The tannic acid in the tea has an astringent effect and will shrink swollen tissues. You can also grate a raw potato and apply it to the eye area, or cover the puffs with cooling, refreshing cucumber slices. Ice cubes will help shrink puffy eyes.

3. Try this exercise: Roll your eyes and look up, then to the right, then down, then to the left, then up again—as if you were seeing the numbers on a giant clock. Really "stretch" your eye muscles as far as they will go in each direction. This "eye calisthenic" will stretch and relax the muscles in the eye area, and may help the sluggish fluids move out.

Steppin' Out: The Nightbird Facial

Here's a superspecial body-involvement facial for on-the-town evenings when you want your face to look better than best. Allow forty-five minutes for this guaranteed radiance treatment.

1. *Animation Exercises for a Come-alive Face*

These simple exercises will relax your face and bring fresh blood into the head and neck area. They will give you more energy for the big evening ahead and help improve skin tone.

The Half Shoulder Stand

Stand on your shoulders with your feet in the air, supporting your lower back with your hands. Keep your feet close together and your back and legs as straight as possible. When you are comfortable in this position, drop your back slightly so that your waist is resting in your hands and your feet and legs are at an angle instead of straight up. This is a yoga posture designed to tone the complexion. Hold the position for at least two minutes.

Neck-relaxing Head Rolls

Tension accumulates in the neck, giving us a tight, not-so-fun-loving expression. To ease the tension, crouch on the floor on your hands and knees, put the top of your head on the floor and roll it, pressing the entire surface of your skull into the floor. Feel all the bumps and contours of your head (and headaches) pressing into that floor. Let the floor massage your head! This exercise will relax your neck, and stimulate circulation in your hair follicles, too.

Lion Face

Kneel on the floor and stick your tongue out as far as possible, rolling your eyes to the sky at the same time. Exhale, making a loud, lion's roaring sound. Release your frustration! Tell off your boss! Roar! When you are finished roaring, try to squeeze all your features into a single point toward your nose. Your face will feel relaxed after this exercise, and you will feel calmer and more cheerful—ready to enjoy. Your face will also look more animated and alive.

2. *Carrot Soufflé Icy Refining Facial*

This extra special facial will refine the texture of your skin and give you a "cool" glow for evening.

1. Put one cut-up carrot in the blender jar and blend thoroughly. Add the juice of half a lemon, one tablespoon of fresh cream, one egg yolk, and blend. Mix in a tablespoon of honey (optional) and let the mixture stand for five minutes. Pat mixture on your face (it will tend to slide off, so make sure you're standing over a sink) and leave on for fifteen minutes. Rinse off with cool water. This recipe makes enough masque for two applications; you can refrigerate the extra.

2. Crush ice cubes and place them in a plastic bag. Hold the bag with a hand towel so your fingers won't freeze, and apply it to your face. This cold pack will shock your face alive and help to close pores. If you don't feel like crushing the cubes, simply put a hand towel in the freezer of your refrigerator until it is icy cold and apply that to your face. If your skin is dry or delicate, skip this step.

3. Pat skin dry with a towel, apply moisturizer and makeup.

ALL-BODY SKIN CARE

A baby almost always has soft, caressable skin—down to his little brown feet. His mother bathes him, powders him, smooths him with lotions, and protects his fragile skin from the wind and sun. Giving your own skin the same high-caliber baby care will make it smoother and softer and invite others to touch it, too. Don't forget about the "invisible" skin you don't always see in the mirror—the person most important to you will see and caress every inch.

The Barbara Walden Luxury Bath

A bath provides me with a chance to relax, and I mean *really* relax. I run a tub of very hot water, douse it with bubble bath and bath oil. Then I turn the radio to soothing music and submerge myself up to the neck. The hot water lets my stiff muscles—tense from a day of traveling, speaking to groups, or standing around in department stores—give up their sore, achy tension. I like to sit in the bath and read short stories, or go over a bit of very lightweight business. I've made sure my bathroom itself is a perfect relaxation room—that everything in it pleases my eye and gives me that "Star" feeling. The floors are carpeted, antique prints hang on the walls, and pretty green plants spill out of the lovely old teapots I've collected for years. I also love beautiful, sensuous towels and bright colors and wallpaper in this all-important spa. After my bath I lubricate my skin with a deep, penetrating body lotion, because the skin on the body has fewer oil glands than the skin on the face and needs extra antidrying protection.

Cleopatra Milk Bath

Every now and then I indulge in a special, luxurious skin-softening bath by putting the contents of two entire quarts of milk in the full tub. There's no guarantee that this highly extravagant bath softens my skin, but if it was good enough for an Egyptian queen, it's good enough for Barbara! One quart of milk, scented with your favorite perfume or bath oil, will do. (You can also substitute economical powdered milk.) Try buttermilk, a superrich dairy smoother, too.

Japanese-style Ache-relieving Bath

Beautiful ladies in Japan are experts in the art of bathing. To bathe Japanese style, wash your body in the shower first, letting the running water take the dirt away. Then draw a bath as hot as you can stand it. If your muscles are really sore, dissolve Epsom salts in the water according to the directions on the package. Sit and soak for at least half an hour. This is a cleaner, more relaxing way to bathe than the western style, or so say the Japanese.

Dry-skin Bath

Unscented castor oil makes an excellent bath oil for dry skin. Use a quarter of a cup in a full tub. Dry-skin victims should avoid very hot bath water; make yours tepid. When you emerge apply moisturizing lotion to your wet skin (the water on your body will help the lotion spread and penetrate) and blot (not rub) yourself dry.

Sour Cream Shower

For a softer skin, rub rich sour cream into your body before you take a shower, then let the water rinse it away. (Don't use soap.)

HERITAGE SECRETS

Fragrant Indian Bath Oil

Women from the subcontinent of India have always used deliciously scented oils to anoint their bodies and hair. Sesame oil, fragrant with pungent spices, was a great favorite for its rich lubricating qualities. You can make a sesame bath oil, similar to that used in ancient India, by purchasing a light, refined sesame oil from your health-food store. Pour it into a clean, wide-mouthed jar and add a teaspoon of whole nutmeg, whole cloves, cardamom seeds, and two sticks of cinnamon (cinnamon soothes the skin). Let the sweet-smelling spices seep into the oil for at least a week, then strain the mixture and add liberally to your bath water.

Flake-removing Rub

Before you take a bath or shower, rub your entire body briskly with a dry hand towel. The mild friction from the towel will gently loosen dry-skin flakes so that they can float away in the water, and will stimulate circulation in the skin as well. For an additional circulation bracer, try an ice-cold shower.

Smoothing the Skin with Hair Removal

Though a little extra hair on the arms, legs, face, and stomach is normal (some even consider it sexy), you may find your smooth-skin image marred by more hair than you like. For centuries, ladies have removed body hair to look as smooth and feminine as possible. In ancient India and Egypt, hair was scraped away with a pumice stone, and depilatories, too, have been around for a long time. Here are some alternative techniques for modern hair removal.

Shaving

The fastest way to remove hair is to shave it. Some people believe that shaving makes body hair thicker and stimulates its rate of growth. This is strictly myth and fairy tale. The hair may *appear* to be thicker when it's first growing in because the stubble is stiff like a bristle; but when it grows out completely, it won't be any thicker than before. Shaving the face, however, is not recommended because the stubble will give you that "Marlboro Man" look.

Waxing

When you wax away excess hair, it takes a while to grow in because you've pulled it out by the roots. The best waxing service, with a minimum of pain, is done by experts in a salon. Hot wax is applied to the hairy area, and when it cools it is stripped off, zipping the hair off with it. You can buy wax for hair removal and use it at home, but be aware that waxing is a tricky process. (One friend of mine tried to wax her underarms and couldn't remove the wax, much less the hair.) Read the directions very carefully and test the wax on a small area of the place you want to strip of hair. Be careful not to overheat the wax (painful burns can be the price) and always pull it off in the opposite direction from the one in which the hair grows. (Note: Cold waxes are available but they are not as effective.) You can remove hair from any part of the body with wax. Beware of blemishes and skin irritations that may result.

Depilatories

Depilatories are for removing hair on the arms and legs, and are most effective on thin, fine hair. Never leave a depilatory on your skin longer than the manufacturer recommends. Test the depilatory before using it; if you see signs of irritation, you may be allergic to that brand.

Electrolysis

The only way to remove hair permanently is via the expensive and uncomfortable process of electrolysis. In electrolysis, a needle is inserted into the hair follicle, and an electric current is sent into it which destroys the root of the hair. Because each hair must be zapped individually and no one can stand too long a session of electrolysis, it takes many appointments to remove hair the electric way. For this reason hair on the arms and legs is seldom removed through electrolysis; it is, however, one of the best ways to remove troublesome facial hair. Some hairs will grow back because the needle did not quite touch the root, and new hairs may begin close to the site of the one you just removed. Before you remove hair from a mole with electrolysis, you should consult your doctor. Hyperpigmentation may also result from electrolysis.

Abnormal Hair Growth

Most of the time excess body hair is caused by hereditary factors (experts say that, in general, black people are less hairy than white people), but certain medications (like those for arthritis) and hormonal disturbances (including menopause) can also inspire the growth of excess hair. If you suspect your sudden growth of hair is abnormal, see your physician.

2

The Barbara Walden
Complete Makeup

WE HAVE A SPECIAL BEAUTY

The days when we were brainwashed into believing that beauty did not come in the shape of a black woman are gone, along with the days when we had to tell ourselves "black is beautiful." Today, we *know* we count high in the ranks of the world's beautiful women, and the world knows it, too. We see our faces on television, on movie screens, and in the pages of all the high-style fashion magazines. The new cosmetics designed especially for us are now part of our special beauty. Applied in the right shades with the right know-how, they emphasize our full, sensuous lips, the bridge of our fabulous noses, our dark, expressive eyes, and bring out the glowing undertones of our skin.

WE'VE COME A LONG WAY

When I first began my own cosmetic business, all makeup on the market was designed for the non-black woman. When we put on the foundations with pink undertones, we looked as if we'd fallen into a flour bin. The lipstick colors were passable, but many of us didn't want to emphasize lips we still considered unattractively large. Then I had a hard time convincing my customers that those full lips were a true beauty trademark. Older women told me the only makeup they'd ever used was a little cheek color, and some told me they made their own by wetting red crepe paper and taking the color from that for their cheeks. My own grandmother ground bricks together and used the orangy powder to bring out her pretty skin tones. We were always gorgeously dressed, and we spent a fortune styling our hair, but when it came to makeup, we wore little or none at all because there wasn't any for us to use.

My cosmetics were among the first to be tailored for the black woman. Now most cosmetic companies are aware of the large market we represent and have provided us with many lines of products designed to match our special beauty. It's about time! Today we have careers and social lives that make us highly visible; naturally, we want our beauty to be visible, too.

THE 1980's LOOK

Believe me, the most beautiful women in the world look more beautiful with makeup. One famous black actress I know told me she once ran to the supermarket in Beverly Hills without a stitch of cosmetics on her face. As she was getting some vegetables out of the frozen food section, she overheard two shoppers trying to decide who she was. The first said, "That's so-and-so!" and the other declared, "No way! So-and-so is much prettier. This is just a poor look-alike." While the two ladies continued to debate whether it was her or not, my actress friend made a silent resolution that she would never step out her door again without putting her face together. This story has a moral in it for all of us: No one ever wants to be just a "poor look-alike" of her most beautiful self! Personally, I wouldn't go out to work in my garden without wearing makeup, because I've learned that the moments when I want or *need* to look my best are never totally predictable.

Makeup enhances every woman's personal beauty, highlights her best features, and softens her flaws. The days of the clean, scrubbed, "natural" look are part of the past, and I, for one, am glad. In my opinion, "natural" and "beautiful" are not necessarily the same thing. The 1980's are asking us to spend more time on our wardrobes, hair, and faces. We are dressing in feminine clothes and styling our hair more elaborately. Our contemporary makeup look is carefully thought out and planned. We're willing to experiment with dramatic new cosmetic shades and techniques, and sculpt our faces with color to match our new, total style.

A MAKEUP TIMETABLE

Beauty has no number. Makeup can help every woman look her best, but how much and what kind she should wear change with her age. A young girl should not start wearing makeup until she is seventeen or eighteen. More than a little lip gloss on a young teenager is unflattering; too much makeup ages her in an unpleasant way, making her look coarse and hard. Skin care should be her number one priority. A woman in her twenties should apply makeup with a lighter touch and in softer shades than a woman in her thirties or forties. As you reach maturity, you can use more cosmetics in more vivid shades to highlight the dramatic planes of your face and to soften down the little wrinkles and creases that begin to appear. In your late fifties and sixties the colors you use should again become more subtle. No woman, I believe, should ever totally abandon her dressing table. Even in the senior retirement years, makeup is still an essential ingredient in an attractive look.

THE BARBARA WALDEN COMPLETE MAKEUP

In the following pages I will tell you how to apply a Complete Makeup in ten steps. I developed this on-the-job-until-evening look for myself and my customers during my years in the cosmetic business. My Complete Makeup carries me anywhere—to a business meeting, to a department store for a promotion campaign, to the grandest lunch with a foreign dignitary, to a senior citizen residence, or to a job-training program where I teach cosmetic skills to women of all ages. At night I freshen my lipstick and blot my foundation with a tissue and let my Complete Makeup carry me to dinner in a favorite restaurant.

I will tell you how to select the right cosmetics, how to apply them, and what tools to use. I will give you some special tips I have learned from handling cosmetics all these years. Later, I will tell those of you who still prefer (or must wear) a minimum of cosmetics how to tone down The Complete Makeup for a natural look that travels even out of doors. I will also tell you how to intensify your daytime makeup for a dazzling nighttime face. Finally, I'll teach you how to use makeup to redesign parts of your face you wish were a little different. Once you learn my techniques and have the right tools and cosmetics at your fingertips, it should take you only fifteen minutes to put on a very 1980 face that you won't have to take off until bedtime.

Before you start, please remember that applying makeup is an art that has been practiced by women since ancient times. When you sit down at your dressing table, don't leave your sense of color, design, and original ideas behind; you are the artist and your face is the canvas. You should bring your imagination and discretion to designing your face, altering the amount and shades of the makeup I suggest to suit your age and personal preference.

The Essentials

1. A Sketch of Your Face

Before you begin to apply makeup, take a good look at your face in the mirror. You may have been applying makeup in an unflattering way for years because you never bothered to take a hard, objective look at the palette. Identify the shape of your face by sketching its outline on paper, erasing when necessary and resketching to get the shape right. Photographs may help you more than the mirror. Is your face long, oval, heart-shaped, or round? If you were Mother Nature, how would you improve on the shape? Where are your cheekbones? Feel the bones with your fingers. How long are they? Where do they begin? Where do they stop? Sketch in your eyes, noting their shape and the way they are set into your face. Try to draw the shape of your lips, noticing whether the corners turn up or down, the irregularities, the curves. Check out the shade of your complexion. Can you discern orange, red, green, blue, or yellow tones in it? As you sketch and observe, try to rid yourself of misconceptions about the way you look. See your face the way you would see the face of a friend. This clear picture will help you when you begin to "paint" and later when I teach you how to redesign flaws with makeup.

2. A Clean, Moisturized Skin

Your skin should be perfectly clean before you apply makeup. After you have faithfully followed my basic cleansing program, apply your moisturizer with clean hands and let it sink in for five minutes before you put on foundation. If you apply foundation immediately, the cosmetic instead of your skin will absorb the moisturizer. The moisturizer must be absorbed in order to provide a barrier between the skin and makeup pigments. If your skin is extremely oily, try patting an astringent on over the moisturizer and letting it wait five minutes, too. Your foundation will spread smoothly over this astringent-moisturizer base, and your face will stay oil-free longer.

3. The Right Light

The perfect lighting for makeup application is daylight. Natural daytime light reveals your good features as well as your flaws and tells you if you've blended your cosmetics correctly so they look smooth and natural. Soft, flattering lights may make you look better in your own mirror, but they won't reveal the truth others will see. If you don't have a dressing table near a window, invest in a makeup mirror illuminated by daytime bulbs. Natural light is also essential for the correct application of evening makeup. It will point out the excess or poorly blended cosmetics that may look fine by candlelight but will be painfully obvious when you step into a brightly lighted elevator or hall. The makeup you leave your home wearing should look good anywhere.

4. The Right Products

Always select a makeup product with as much care as you'd take in choosing a blouse or a pair of shoes. Cosmetics are one of your most important fashion accessories. Many ladies come rushing up to my counter on their lunch hour and say, "Give me a lipstick, please." I insist that the customer slow down, choose carefully, and take home a product she truly loves. If you are just beginning to use makeup or don't trust your color sense, have a professional makeup artist help you make your selections. If you are buying an individual cosmetic, like a new lipstick or eye-shadow, tell the makeup artist what other cosmetic colors you want to wear with it. Some shades of rouge look best with some shades of lipstick, and eye colors can be chosen to complement each other as well as your skin. If you take the time, you will discover product shades that flatter your face in ways you never dreamed possible. After I've helped a lady choose a dramatic new shade of lipstick or eye color, I often hear her say, "I never would have picked that gorgeous color myself!"

The best cosmetics are not necessarily the most expensive. However, it is important to try a sample before you buy. A cosmetic may look fine in the package, but not feel, smell, or spread the way you like. Even the least expensive brand costs too much when it doesn't work for you.

THE TEN STEPS

You are now ready to begin The Complete Makeup. Read all the information on each step carefully before you purchase cosmetics or begin to apply them.

Step 1: Foundation

Your foundation is the backbone and the soul of your makeup. I like to call it "your second skin." The right foundation will bring out the exciting undertones in your complexion—the beautiful orange, blue, red, green, or yellow lights that make your skin come alive. The black woman is lucky because she never has to apply two or three different shades of foundation to her skin to enhance and even out its natural tone as many white women do; one carefully selected foundation will do the job. Foundation also evens out the irregularities in the skin's surface and conceals minor flaws. When you are wearing the right foundation, people will never say, "I like your makeup," they will exclaim, "Oh, what have you done to your skin!"

Selecting a Product

The foundation color that's right for you may look very different from the shade of your skin. The right foundation will contain the same undertones that your skin does; but whereas those colors may be more or less invisible in your skin, they will be more obvious in a foundation. Many very dark-skinned ladies, for example, refuse to believe they have the color blue in their skin, but when those blue tones are emphasized with a foundation that has a blue base, they look gorgeous. If your skin has orange undertones, you will want to select a foundation to bring out the tones. For these reasons it is difficult to select the right foundation without the help of a trained makeup artist who knows what product will match your skin. Making the correct selection is really important because none of your other makeup will look right if the foundation is wrong. If you choose a pink-toned foundation made for light-skinned women, your complexion will look ashy or gray. If you choose the wrong foundation shade in a black cosmetic line, you will look like you're wearing a mask. Have the makeup artist put the foundation sample on your chinline and blend it up onto your face. If you don't see a line and the foundation blends with your neck tones, you have selected the right shade.

Never-Never Number One

Never let a salesperson test foundation on the inside of your arm, wrist, or on the back of your hand. The skin tone and texture of your arm or hand are completely different from those of your face.

Correcting Skin Tones

Avoid selecting a foundation to make your skin lighter or darker, or one that declares war on your basic undertones. These foundations will not change the color of your skin; they will only advertise the fact that you are wearing makeup. Always work *with* your basic skin tones for the best results.

There are two tones I sometimes see in black skin that are not attractive. One is a grayish hue that can be corrected with a bronze-toned foundation. A very few black women have a harsh reddish cast to the skin; a beige-toned foundation will improve this.

Many black women have a lot of acid in their skin, which causes foundation to turn a shade darker right away. If this happens to you, buy foundation that is one shade lighter than the one you actually need. Your skin will tend to darken as you get older; when this occurs, you will need a new, darker foundation.

Choosing the Right Formula

Prepare yourself for some controversial information! I believe that no matter what type of skin you have—oily, normal, or dry—you should wear an oil-based foundation. We have all been led to believe that if our skin is oily, a water-based makeup is a must. I, like everyone else, used to think that the oil in oil-based makeup would clog my pores and make my skin break out. Yet the water-based foundation I wore made my skin feel "tight," and showed every pore, tiny hairline, and crease. The oil in my skin broke through this chalky foundation and formed little beads. When I began to design my own cosmetics, I tried several different water-based formulas with no positive results. I told my chemist, "To me, none of this looks right." He said, "I'd like to try an oil base on your oily skin." I told him my dermatologist had forbidden me to wear any makeup with oils in it. He said, "We can only try it and see what happens." He made up a sample and it was perfect—I wish I could relive that happy moment! Gone were the aging effect of the water-based makeup, the tight feeling, and the little oil beads. The foundation looked terrific and did not make my skin break out. We had proved that oil and water just don't mix.

Today my line of cosmetics does not include any water-based foundations. I believe that foundations must contain oils in order to blend naturally with the surface of the skin. The oil glands produce too much oil in some people because of internal problems, not because of the makeup they wear. If you have oily skin and are prone to blemishes, stick with an oil-based foundation, but take extra care to clean and treat your skin properly after you remove your makeup. If you suffer from recurrent acne, see a dermatologist and only wear foundation on special occasions until your condition has improved. When the oil in your skin begins to form a film on top of the foundation, blot it with a tissue as I do; this immediately restores the clean finish to your makeup.

Choosing the Right Texture

Foundation comes in many textures, including creams, foams, and liquids. My personal favorite is the cream-type foundation, which works best on most of my customers' skin. Some ladies prefer a liquid. If you are just starting to wear makeup, you will find the cream-type foundation is easier to work with because you have more control over how much you put on. You may be surprised to learn that the cream foundation is also sheerer than the liquid type. When you have chosen the right shade and type, play around with the product before you buy it. Rub it between your fingers and test it on your face for spreadability—how does it blend, how light is it, how easily does it move around? Foundation should never be stiff, or runny, or so thick it totally camouflages your natural skin tones.

The Tools

The best tools for applying foundation are your own fingers. Fingers gently stimulate circulation and their body heat helps spread the foundation smoothly on your face. Your fingers have another major plus—they are easy to keep clean and sanitary. I don't believe in using cosmetic sponges to apply foundation, because busy ladies just don't take the time to wash them carefully after each application. Most use the same old sponge and keep putting the same old bacteria and stale makeup pigments back on their faces.

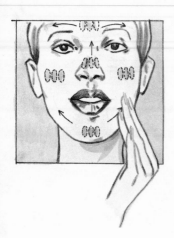

The Technique

Make sure your hands are clean. Take a small amount of the cream foundation on your second finger. If you are using a liquid, shake it well and take what you need from the cap. Use your finger to place a dot of foundation on your forehead, both cheeks, nose, and chin. Blend it in with light strokes up and out—every place except in the eye socket and on the neck. Stop at your chinline. No one needs foundation on her neck; the proper shade will blend with your neck tones. Foundation applied to the neck will end up on your collars, and will result in higher dry-cleaning bills. Be sure to blend your foundation thoroughly—it should look like part of your skin, not a coat sitting on top. If you have blemishes or imperfections, add a touch of extra makeup over them when the basic job is done.

Step 2: Contour Shading

Contour shading is an essential step in the Complete Makeup—especially for the black woman. Contouring creams blend in well with our dark skin tones, look natural, and give the illusion that our faces are slimmer and more pefectly shaped and our bones more dramatically striking. Contour shading is for every day, not only special occasions. With a little practice, contouring is easy and quick to apply, and will give your makeup an elegant, professional touch.

Selecting a Product

Contour shadings are creams that are slightly darker than your regular foundation. They are made in only a few shades for the dark-skinned woman, so selection is easy. The two shades in my line suit every customer we've ever had. The contouring cream should be soft and spread easily.

The Tools

Your fingers.

The Technique

Basically, any area of your face that you want to hollow out should be shadowed with the contouring cream. The shadowed area will recede or become less visible, and the part of your face next to the shadowed area will stand out more. Look at the sketch of your face and decide what areas you'd like to soften or emphasize. Because an oval face is a classic sign of beauty, you will probably want your face to appear as much like an oval as possible. The areas you should shade are the ones you consider too long, square, or round to contribute to the ideal shape. Even if

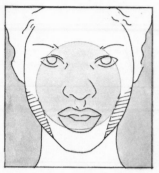

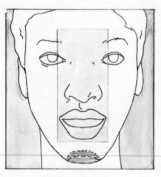

your face is already beautifully shaped, contouring will give it a slimmer, high-fashion look and make your cheekbones seem higher and bonier. You may also want to use contouring cream to emphasize the bridge of your nose. Before you begin, remember that contouring is a way to give the illusion of reshaping the face. Many of the most famous models (like Beverly Johnson) have heart-shaped faces, and some very glamorous ladies also have faces that are long, round, or square.

If your face is round . . . Suck in your cheeks hard. The hollow that forms beneath your cheekbones and just below the top row of teeth is the area where you will put contour shading. Apply a dot or two of shading to the hollow area with your forefinger and blend it in, beginning from the earlobe and stroking down to the jawline. Do the other side. This technique will make any face seem slimmer and the cheekbones more prominent.

If your face is long and thin . . . You can make it look shorter by contouring your chin. Apply a touch of shading to the tip of the chin and blend with downward strokes.

If your face is square-jawed . . . If the bones of your jawline are prominent, apply the shading to the tip of those bones and blend it in.

If your face is heart-shaped . . . If you have a wide forehead and a narrow chin, blend the contouring cream into your temples and into each side of your forehead. This will make the cheekbones seem more prominent and de-emphasize the triangular shape of your face.

To emphasize the bridge of the nose . . . Contouring the nose will highlight its special beauty. Place a dot of the contouring cream at the inner corner of each eye. Blend down both sides of your nose and around the wings on both sides. Make sure the contouring forms a straight line on either side.

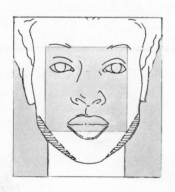

CAUTION! Remember, you want your contouring to provide the most delicate illusion. Apply the cream sparingly to your face. Too much will make your skin look dirty. The dot of shading you begin with should be tiny and create only the faintest shadow. In daylight your contour shading should be no more obvious than foundation. Practice the techniques at the dressing table before you make your debut.

Step 3: Cream Rouge

Cream rouge emphasizes your cheekbones and complements the pretty tones of your skin. Do not confuse it with powder blush, which has a less intense color tone and should be used to add highlights to your face.

Selecting a Product

There is no single shade of cream rouge that is the only one for you. Many will blend with the tones of your skin. You can have a wardrobe of several colors and wear them according to your mood and the other makeup colors you are using. Plums, burgundies, deep reds, and brick tones all look well on the black woman. Avoid pink rouges, or very pale colors, which won't be deep enough to add color to your face. The texture of the rouge should be soft and light in consistency, and should blend easily and smoothly on your skin. Never buy a product you have to struggle to get on your face. I prefer a cream rouge to the liquid type, because the amount you put on your cheeks is easier to gauge and control.

The Tools

Your fingers. Always wash your fingers, or clean them with a tissue, when you move from one makeup product to another.

The Technique

Feel your cheekbones with your fingers so you know where they begin and end and what shape they have. Smile and notice how your cheeks make two round balls. Apply a dab of rouge with your fingertip to the top of the ball of your cheek and blend it out toward your hairline. The color should be most intense on the

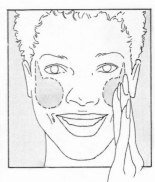

ball of the cheek and fade out toward the hairline. Take a pencil and place it out from your nostril in a straight line. Your rouge should never fall below this line.

Step 4: Face Powder

Many ladies consider face powder old-fashioned and stopped wearing it years ago. Recently, face powder has been revived with good reasons. It seals your makeup, helping it to stay on all day, provides a smooth finish, and minimizes the size of your pores.

Selecting a Product

Translucent face powder gives darker skins an unpleasant gray tinge. Choose a sheer but tinted powder that blends with your complexion tones and your foundation. It is best to purchase face powder in a sprinkle-top can, or transfer it to an empty talcum powder container or a saltcellar with large holes in the cap.

The Tools and the Technique

The best way to put on face powder is with a fabric puff. These puffs come several to a package and can be washed in the sink or thrown in the washing machine when they are soiled. Sprinkle the powder on the puff, fold the puff over, and rub the powder into it. Open the puff up and shake it to get rid of the excess. Then lightly pat your entire face, using gentle, stroking motions. I prefer a puff to a brush because it makes it easier to get the right amount of powder on your face. If you prefer a brush, select a large one with soft bristles. Sprinkle a little powder on a tissue, dab the brush on the powder, shake it to get off the excess, then brush it on lightly with upward motions.

Never-Never Number Two

The secret of powdering is to apply the minimum amount to your face. Less is better than more. Never overpowder or reapply it during the day. One application should be enough. Too much powder can give you a chalky, grainy look. Never grind or rub the powder into your face; use a feather touch. Never put powder beneath your eye socket—it will get into the tiny hairlines in this area and emphasize them.

Step 5: Eyebrow Shaping

Your eyebrows are one of your most important features. I like to say, "They set the stage of your face," because all by themselves these mobile lines express various moods and emotions. It is important to shape eyebrows correctly. Improperly drawn or shaped brows can communicate negative emotions. Half-moons can make you look sad. Eyebrows that turn up at the ends make you look frightened. Eyebrows that meet in the middle can make you look fierce. Everyone's brows should be arched in the center, have gently tapering ends, and look as natural as possible.

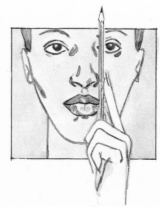

The Art of Tweezing

Before you use a pencil on your brows, you will want to train and shape them with a tweezer. Once your eyebrows are correctly shaped, plucking a few stray hairs every other day will save you an hour of agonizing surgery once a month. Before you begin to tweeze, take a pencil and place the eraser end at the bridge of your nose. The pencil will make a straight line up past your eyebrow to your forehead. The place where the pencil falls is where your eyebrow should begin. You will want to tweeze hairs that grow beyond this point toward the space between your eyes. (My eyebrows originally met together like John L. Lewis's!) Now, look straight ahead and place the pencil directly in front of the center of your eye (where the pupil is). Where the pencil touches your brow is where the arch should be. Finally, put the pencil at the wing of your nose and extend it, at a forty-five-degree angle, to the corner of your eye. The brow should not extend beyond the pencil line.

To numb the areas you are going to tweeze, freeze them with an ice cube or apply some rubbing alcohol with cotton. Always pluck the hairs in the direction in which they grow. When you are "arching" the brow, pluck hairs from underneath. When you are finished, clean the area carefully with freshener or alcohol, and don't apply eye makeup for several hours. Don't overdo the tweezing or try to make your brows too thin or precise. You

should be able to live with the brows you design. If you pluck the same hair over a period of years, it may not grow back. Remember, the more natural brow is now more in style than the very thin, severely arched one.

Never-Never Number Three

Never shave your eyebrows with a razor blade. The blade can slip, and you can commit suicide in the name of beauty. Shaved hairs will also grow back more rapidly (because you didn't pluck the hair at its root) and more coarsely, leaving a dark, unattractive "shadow" like a man's beard.

Shaping With a Pencil

Even if your hair and skin are very dark, always choose a brown pencil for your brows. A black pencil has an aging effect—nothing will put ten years on you faster than coal-black brows. You can select a cosmetic eyebrow pencil or get a soft gray-brown pencil from an art-supply store. The pressure you apply to the brown pencil will make the color more or less intense. Sharpen the pencil well and feather in lines wherever your own brows are scanty; the tiny lines should look as much like real hairs as possible. Only use the pencil to fill in gaps between your eyebrow hairs, not to "draw" the brow itself. Your basic brow shape should be formed by tweezing. When you are finished penciling, brush the brows with a child's toothbrush to make them look smooth and natural.

Step 6: Eye Color

The beautiful shades of shadow and pencil now available can give your eyes drama, highlighting their expression and shape with special allure. Your eye makeup can be subtle or extravagant, simple or complex, depending on the time you have to spend, the places you're going, and your mood. Eye color gives you a chance to use your individual sense of design and artistic skill. Always bring your imagination to your eye makeup. Don't depend totally on my suggestions. Your eye shape and tone, skin color, and imagination should help guide your artistic decisions. Loosen up and have a ball with eye color! You may find you enjoy designing special color motifs for your eyes in spare moments.

Selecting the Product

Eye colors come in cream, powder, and liquid form, and also as soft pencils which can be used to both shadow and contour the eye. Cream shadows are good for dry or mature skin, and blend sheerly and naturally into the eyelid. If your cream shadow gets into the creases of your eyelid and forms lines, dab a little talcum powder on the lid before you apply the shadow and blot the color after application. Powder shadows are easy to work with and come in an amazing variety of colors. They are also the most economical of the color shadows because they last the longest in the container. Sometimes, however, they give a grainy appearance unless you take care to blend them well. Eye pencils come in many subtle color tones and are convenient to carry and use. They help you shape your eyelid as well as color it. The pencil should be easy to apply. If it seems "stiff" or hard, run the tip through hot tap water for a second to soften it. If the pencil is too soft, run it through cold water. Liquid shadows are sheer and long-lasting on the eyelid, and often flatter the mature eye, which has developed loose skin on the lid; but they offer a rather limited color selection and tend to dry out in the tubes. You can easily combine any of the eye-color products. Which you use and when you use it is largely a matter of personal preference.

Choosing Colors

The black woman can wear eye colors in rainbow hues—the many vivid purples, soft violet and plum shades, bright blues and subtle teal blues, greens, blue-grays, lavender-grays, charcoal-grays, and green-grays, soft browns, platinums, golds, coppers, and bronzes. Recently I've found that even pink and salmon tones flatter our skin. Very dark-skinned ladies with blue tones in their skin look fabulous in pearl-grays. There are a few colors, however, that are not for us: The hard browns and blacks tend to make us look like we have two black eyes. Frosted hues are best used at night or just to add the faintest sparkle to daytime eyes, since they don't give the eyes as much depth as matte colors. Shiny eyeshadows also emphasize signs of aging on the eyelid.

Because the majority of us have brown eyes (in various shades and intensities), we should choose shadows to emphasize the white of our eyes. In general, the shadows should blend with our skin tones and help reveal their hidden lights. Don't choose eye colors to match the outfit you're wearing. This is an old-fashioned approach. If green eyeshadow looks great with your skin, it will look equally great with a blue dress. Think of eye color as a fashion accessory, used to complement your wardrobe. In fact, eyeshadow colors that are flattering to you are often the same you wear well in clothes. Though you need only one foundation, one powder, one eyebrow pencil, one contouring cream, and, at most, a few cream rouges, you may want to have as many exciting eye makeup colors in your cosmetic wardrobe as you can afford. I love to change eye color according to my whim. You'll almost never catch Barbara with less than three colors on her eyes, blended and smoothed into an intriguing painting.

The Tools

You need a sharpener to keep eye pencils honed to a dull point. Q-Tips are useful for blending creams or pencil colors. You can apply powders with a special soft-bristled brush. I don't care for the little sticks with sponges on the end, as they can seldom be kept clean enough. Anything you put on your eyes should be as sanitary as possible, because eyes are susceptible to bacterial infections. Clean your shadow brush with a little skin freshener or alcohol. If you work with your fingers, make sure they are clean, too. Ladies with long nails should keep them away from the delicate skin of the eyes, and use tools to apply and blend eye color.

Lining the Eyes

Lining your eyes emphasizes their special shape. Choose a pretty eye pencil and move it in the direction of the outer corner of the eye, drawing a line as close to the lashes as possible. Then smudge it with your finger. Never work the pencil toward the inner corner of the eye because you might stretch the eyelid's fragile skin. If you have extra skin on the eyelid, pull it out with your finger toward the corner of the eye and hold it taut while you draw the line. Add the same smudged line below your lower fringe of lashes. Remember, you want a sexy shadow, not a hard, definite line.

HERITAGE SECRETS

The Beauty of Kohl

Kohl, a dark, silvery mineral, has been powdered and used by many dark-skinned women all over the world to emphasize their eyes. In Ethiopia sloe-eyed beauties keep their kohl in decorative vases and ring their eyes with it every day, using a small stick. Indian women, too, have long applied kohl in symbolic colors (green for plants, yellow for the sun, and red for blood) to decorate their eyes and protect their lids from the sun's bright glare. Kohl has also always been popular with Arab ladies. Today you can buy this time-tested cosmetic in modern form at many counters. The soft kohl pencils (some companies also put out kohl in powders and sticks) are easily smeared and blended into the lid for a sultry, smoky effect. For a special flair try lining the little shelf or the inside of both your upper and lower lids with kohl.

Shadowing the Lid

After you've lined your eyes, take a powder, cream, or liquid shadow, or another pencil, and fill in the lid area up to the crease. You may want to add another color to the crease itself and blend it with your finger or a tool. (A dark shade makes a slightly protruding eye seem to recede, and a light color brings out a deep-set eye). Add the same color, or another color, to the outer corner of the eye and blend it out a bit beyond the corner. Your shadow color should always be most intense toward the outer corner of the eye, and less intense at the inner corner. For the final touch, add a different color to the area of the eyebone just beneath the brow—use pale brown, plum, platinum, or burgundy—and blend it well. I prefer not to use blue, green, or aqua on the eyebone. These colors are not the most attractive on this part of the eye.

 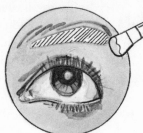

HERITAGE SECRETS

Cleopatra Eyes

Women in ancient Egypt made their dark, almond-shaped eyes seem extra large and luminous by ringing them with kohl and shadowing them with many kinds of ground metallic substances, which beautified them with vivid colors and also protected them from eye diseases common in the hot Nile region. Medicinal shadows made from green malachite, iridescent antimony, and dark galena were painted on the lids and brows with ivory pencils. Different shades of eye color were used for different times of the day and year, according to the quality of natural light. Cleopatra, one of the outstanding dark-skinned beauties of all time, had a special technique to glorify her eyes. For a modern version of Cleopatra's Eye Design:

1. Line your upper lid, above the lashes, with a gray or brown, freshly sharpened, soft pencil. Extend the liner beyond the corner of your eye by drawing a small triangular shape, then blurring its outlines slightly with your finger. For a more modified Cleopatra eye, simply extend the liner on your top lid beyond the corner of your eye and smudge.

2. Now apply a blue shadow to the lid, blending the blue into the dark triangle.

3. Line the bottom lid, beneath the bottom lashes, with a vivid green pencil.

4. Use plenty of mascara and emphasize your brows with eyebrow pencil a bit more than usual.

These are the basics for minimum eye makeup technique. Here are some additional interesting suggestions:

• Try lining the lower lid of the eye (beneath the lower lashes) with a different colored pencil than the one you used on the upper lid. The effect is highly dramatic.

• Try a curry- or mustard-colored eyeshadow. This brings out the gold flecks in brown eyes.

• Put a dark shadow on the lid, dust with a little face powder, then add lighter shade over it for an intense color blend.

• Brown shadows and blue eyeliners, or vice versa, are always an interesting combination.

• Add a single dot of vivid color to the midpoint of the eyebone and blend.

• Line the little "shelf" you see when you pull down the lower lid of your eye with a bright color of blue or lavender. This will make the whites of your eyes seem whiter. This technique is for special occasions only; if you use it every day, the makeup may build up on the sensitive inside lid and damage your eye.

• Make your own designer shadows by mixing colors on your eye. Try combining a soft lavender with a warm apricot, greens and aquas, plums and blues, silvers and burgundies. Here's where native artistic talent can shine. Don't be afraid to blend wildly different hues for fabulous effects. Reject "muddy" combinations and always experiment *before* you take your creations out the door—you don't want your eyelids to look like a five-year-old's finger paintings.

Never-Never Number Four

Never let your eye colors go unblended. They shouldn't "sit" on the eye but mold into the texture of the skin. Blending will make them more natural and call attention to your gorgeous eyes and skin, not to the cosmetics themselves. Never use pearlized shades or glittery frosted shadows for business wear unless they are extremely subtle.

Step 7: Mascara

Most lashes need mascara to make a thicker and more luxurious frame for the eyes.

Selecting a Product

Selecting a mascara which stays put and does not irritate your eyes can involve a process of trial and error. The automatic-type mascara, with the tube and brush inside, is the easiest to use. Choose a waterproof mascara which doesn't smear. I prefer the lash-lengthening type with little fibers that catch on the hair of your lashes and make them look longer.

The Tools

You will need a tiny comb, sold at cosmetic counters, to separate your lashes after you have applied the mascara.

The Technique

Never glop loads of sticky mascara on your lashes. Take a minimal amount on the brush applicator and stroke it on from the base of the lashes to the tips. Let it dry, then relax your eye and apply the mascara to the top sides of the lashes. Then brush the applicator across the tips of the lashes. Finally, apply mascara to the fringe of lashes on the lower lid. Repeat the entire process for a more dramatic effect. When the mascara is dry, separate the lashes with the tiny comb to prevent them from sticking together in artificial-looking spikes.

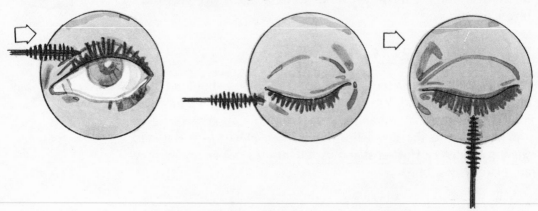

If you get mascara or any bits of eye makeup into your eyes, don't rub your eyes with your hands, no matter how strong the temptation. Rubbing will only embed the troublesome speck in your eye tissue. Instead, let your tears accumulate and wash the speck out of your eye the natural way.

Kitchen Lash Lengthener

Here's an old secret for lengthening your lashes. Dip your forefinger into some cornstarch, then press it into the palm of your hand, leaving a trace of the white powder there. Then take your clean middle finger, dip it into the cornstarch on your palm, and apply a bare trace to your lashes. Apply your mascara over the cornstarch-coated lashes, then separate them carefully with a toothpick or your tiny comb.

Curling and Straightening Lashes

If your lashes are too straight, try using an eyelash curler. After you have applied mascara, press the lashes hard with the curler, relax the pressure, then press again. Curled lashes liven up eyes. Many black women have lashes that are *too* curly. I recommend brushing the unruly lashes regularly with a small brush before you apply mascara. This does wonders for straightening them.

False Lashes for Lashless Ladies

A large percentage of black people have minimal lashes. This is because the hair follicle in the lid that produces our lashes is curved and sends out a very short lash. If you are basically lashless, mascara will not add much allure to your eyes, and you may want to wear false lashes even during the day, carefully trimmed to look natural and not too extravagant. See "Dazzle Lashes" under "Steppin' Out: The Dazzle Look" for instructions on how to apply them.

Step 8: Concealing Circles Beneath the Eyes

Quite a few black women have dark areas beneath their eyes that should be lightened to produce an even complexion. You will also want to apply a special cream makeup under your eyes, because regular foundation is not really made for this part of the face. The eye socket is the first place to show the hairlines that arrive with maturity; any foundation, no matter how creamy, always works its way into these tiny lines and reveals them. Though the concealing cream looks much like your foundation, it contains additional lubricating oils and blends better with the skin beneath the eyes.

Selecting a Product

The special foundation for the eye socket comes in stick or cream form and has many different names: "concealer," "coverup," "eye lightener," and so on. I prefer the cream because it blends in smoothly and easily. Make sure to buy one in a black cosmetic line. All the products for non-black women will make your eye socket too pale and chalky, reversing your problem and giving you white rings under the eyes.

The Tools

Use cotton balls and your fingers, or a stick with a little sponge on the end.

The Technique

First, remove all traces of makeup and foundation from the eye socket with a cotton ball. Then gently pat the concealing cream on the skin beneath the eye without pulling or rubbing this delicate, easily stretched area. If you have long nails, use a clean stick sponge or a Q-Tip and pat on the cream.

Step 9: Lip Color

Your full, sensuous lips are part of your special beauty and should be emphasized. The deep, bright colors designed especially for our lips have become a worldwide trend.

Preparing Your Lips for Color

Before you apply lip color, you will want to even out the shade of your lips. Many of us have one lip that is lighter than the other, or lips that are several shades darker or lighter than the rest of our skin. Our lower lip is often pinker in tone, and the upper lip is dark. Though we don't tend to notice this difference in each other (I have it and so do my two sisters), we notice it in ourselves because it changes the color of the lipstick, making it look as if we are wearing two different colors. In the past we compensated for this color change by putting a different shade of lipstick on one lip than we did on the other. Several companies now make a foundation designed to even out the difference. These products are highly creamy and contain a moisturizer. If your bottom lip is lighter than your top lip, put a little dark lip foundation on the tip of your finger and smooth it out across your bottom lip. Do not blot your lips by rubbing them together. Instead, take a tissue and blot only the lip to which you've applied the lip foundation. Then you can put on lipstick. If both your lips are darker than the rest of your face, you will want to lighten both of them so that your lipstick will remain its true color. Apply a light-colored lip foundation to both lips and blot with a tissue. If the upper and lower lips are too light, apply the darker shade of foundation to both of them, using the same technique.

Many of us have a lot of acid in our skin which changes the color of lipstick. If you have this problem, you can buy a special sealer to prevent the acid from affecting the lipstick. This sealer, often yellow in color, comes in a lipstick tube, and is made by several companies.

Lip Care

Lips are part of your skin and need equally conscientious care. Plain Vaseline, applied at night, keeps lips soft and smooth. Lips can chap in the cold or peel in the sun. Always keep some moisturizer, baby oil, or a Chap Stick on your lips when you are not wearing lipstick. An inexpensive product called Blistex is excellent for curing cold sores. Apply the ointment as soon as you see the impurities surfacing.

Lining Your Lips

Using a lip-lining pencil prevents lipstick from bleeding out beyond the boundaries of your lips and gives them a definite outline. This step is especially important as you get older and the natural outline of the lips becomes less definite.

Selecting a Lip Liner

Lip liners come in pencil form in many shades. The one you choose should be slightly darker than your lipstick, though not necessarily in the same color range. You can, for example, use a burgundy liner with a red lipstick, or a brown liner with an orange lipstick. You can also choose a liner color that's close to the natural tone of your lips, like brown or auburn. Stay away from liners that look black on your lips, however; these look hard and bizarre. Before you buy the liner, test it on the back of your hand to make sure it draws easily.

The Technique

If you are basically happy with the shape of your lips, draw a light line all around your mouth, following its natural outlines. Make the line definite, but not too deep or hard. Later I will tell you how to use the lip-lining pencil to give the illusion that your lips are a different shape or size.

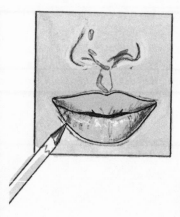

Selecting Lipsticks

Lipsticks are an important fashion accessory, and you can have many in your cosmetic wardrobe, provided they blend with your skin tones. Plums, burgundies, pretty, clear reds, smoky reds with blue or purple tones, oranges, brick tones, browns, dark raspberries, and deep roses are all lovely on the black skin. Rust is especially gorgeous on most black women. Even lavender lipstick looks pretty on our skin. Only very, very pale shades are forbidden colors for the black woman. I tried the whites and pale pinks when they were in fashion, and they made me look embalmed! Unless you are very young, you should also avoid frosted lipstick shades; they emphasize lines and creases in the lower lip of the mature woman.

Always try to test the lipstick sample in the store on your own lips. Tissue the tester off before you touch it to your mouth, or ask the makeup artist at the counter to apply the sample with a clean brush. If you test the lipstick on the back of your hand, you may get some idea of the basic color, but that color will never look the same on your lips, which have an entirely different tone and texture than those of your hand as well as acids that alter the lipstick's shade. If you think your new lipstick is a disaster once you get it home, try wearing it with different eye colors and different clothes. Often a lipstick that looks so-so on a clean, scrubbed face in combination with jeans and a sweatshirt takes on an aura of special glamour when the rest of your makeup complements it, or when you wear it with a fashionable outfit and hairstyle.

Design Your Own Shades

A new lipstick can provide a terrific pick-me-up for your entire face (and frame of mind). However, instead of buying a new lipstick whenever you need a change, try blending the colors you already have. I've been wearing the same orange lipstick for years, but I often take one of the newer shades—the plums, burgundies, and browns (none of which do much for me by themselves)—and apply it over my favorite orange standby. The result: a brand-new designer shade that's just right for me.

The Perils of Lip Gloss

Many black women still feel their lips are too large and don't want to call attention to them. Instead of wearing lipstick they coat their lips with a colorless or very pale gloss. This actually makes the lips look larger—like shiny blobs of grease. I've even seen celebrities make this mistake. Lip gloss can add a pretty sheen to your regular lipstick, but lots of it all by itself looks unattractive. If I can't convince you that your large, full lips are a beauty plus, a gorgeous shade of lipstick might do the job. You might want to try a combination lipstick and gloss, which comes in the same tube, for a softer, natural color.

Choosing the Right Texture

Lipstick should be soft and go on easily, and it should stay on, too. Avoid one that leaves a constant trademark on glasses and coffee cups. Some lipsticks are too soft and tend to melt when your body heat hits them; these come off almost as soon as you put them on. A good lipstick is neither too soft nor too hard. Remember, the Food and Drug Administration has forbidden cosmetic companies to use Red #2 and other harsh dyes in lipstick. Today's safe, gentle dyes are sometimes less durable, and you may have to reapply lip colors more often, no matter what product you buy.

The Tools

Every woman should own a lipstick brush. These soft-bristled brushes let you apply lip color more accurately. When you use a brush, the lipstick goes exactly where you want it to go, and you can work it into your lips so it stays put longer. A lipstick brush is also economical. When the lipstick has worn down to the base of the container, there is still plenty inside the tube, which you can reach with your brush instead of throwing the lipstick away. Lipstick brushes also come in portable styles and fit easily into your purse. I usually apply my lipstick with a brush in the morning (it takes a few extra seconds) and refresh it directly from the tube during the day.

The Technique

After you've lined your lips with the pencil, run your lipstick brush on the side of the lipstick instead of on the tip. This technique keeps the lipstick in a shape you can use without the brush, too. Then carefully brush the color inside the line of your lips, gently blending the lipstick and the line you've drawn with the brush. If you like, add a light touch of gloss or Vaseline over the basic color (but not much!).

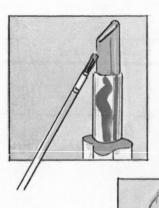

HERITAGE SECRETS

Egyptian Lips

Egyptian ladies used to tint their lips blue. To capture some of the Nile's mysterious allure, use a blue eye-color pencil to line your lips instead of your usual lip-lining pencil. Then apply a plum-colored lipstick, blending the blue outlines well with the lipstick. You may want to add a tint of blue color to your entire mouth with the pencil (or with a blue lipstick; several brands are on the market) and apply a coat of clear red or plum over the top.

Step 10: Powder Blush

The final step of your Complete Makeup is to highlight your face with powder blush—the best way to bring attention to your prettiest planes, bones, and features.

Selecting a Blush

Most blushes have approximately the same texture and consistency, though some leave a deeper color on the skin than others and stay on longer. Deep roses, plums, rust colors, browns, brick, and red tones are all attractive on the black woman. You can have several different blushes in your cosmetic wardrobe, or one favorite.

The Tools

You need a large, soft brush to apply your blush highlighter. You might want to substitute a fine brush from an art-supply store for the one that comes with the blush.

The Technique

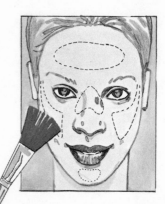

Stroke the blush lightly on the areas you want to highlight. Don't put too much of the cosmetic on the brush. Decide which areas of your face you'd like to emphasize. Blush is pretty on the bridge of your nose, your chinline, and your forehead. Try stroking it in a triangle shape on the cheeks, then carry it up around the eyebone to give your face a slim, fashionable look. You can also use your blush to emphasize the areas you've sculpted earlier with contour shading.

BARBARA'S SIX-STEP NATURAL LOOK OR THE I-HATE-TO-WEAR-MAKEUP LOOK

There are many women who still resist makeup—some for religious reasons, some because they've never worn it before and don't know how to apply it, and some because the men in their lives don't like to see them in makeup. (Have you ever noticed he doesn't like it on you, but admires other women who wear it?) For those who have reasons for wearing as little makeup as possible, but want some of the beautiful benefits, I've designed a special Six-Step Natural Look for beginners and conscientious objectors. This Natural Look is also good for senior citizens, and girls approaching their twenties, who want the softest makeup possible.

Step 1: Foundation

Foundation is a must for the black woman, no matter how natural she wants her face to be. Even if you wear no other makeup at all, you should apply foundation over your usual moisturizer. Foundation does much more for us than for the non-black woman, who does not have the many subtle undertones our foundation helps reveal. Foundation, more than any other cosmetic, brightens our faces and makes them come alive. Follow the directions for applying foundation in the section entitled The Barbara Walden Complete Makeup, but use less and blend it out thoroughly. Don't apply too much; keep it as natural as possible, letting your skin show through.

Step 2: Powder

Powder, too, is a must. It sets and seals the foundation. Follow the instructions given in The Complete Makeup.

Step 3: Eye Color

Skip lining your eyes and simply apply a soft violet shade, or a pretty salmon-colored powder or cream shadow to the entire eyelid. You can stop the shadow at the crease or continue it up to the eyebone. You may also use a pencil to shadow the eyes in these colors, which look very natural on our skin, enhancing the eyes without calling attention to the cosmetics themselves. Try several violet shades at a cosmetic counter until you've found the one that looks most natural with your complexion.

Step 4: Coverup for Under-eye Circles

You will need a covering cream for the area under your eyes, as your regular foundation is not the appropriate cosmetic for this part of your face. See the directions in The Complete Makeup.

Step 5: Lip Color

Choose a lipstick in the softest plum shade you can find. Many black women think brown lipsticks look more natural with their skin tones, but brown actually becomes a strong, sometimes hard color on our dark skin. Plum shades always look the most natural, and there are many different plum tones available. Don't line your lips. Simply apply the lipstick from the tube or with a lipstick brush, following the natural outlines of your mouth. If you, or someone in your life, is strongly opposed to makeup, eliminate the lipstick and substitute a little moisturizer or lip conditioner on the lips to keep them soft and moist. Lipstick is the cosmetic most easily identified as "makeup."

Step 6: Powder Blush

A touch of powder blush in a deep rose shade is pretty and natural. Smile and brush it lightly on the balls of your cheeks and up and around the eyebone if you like. Always brush the blusher out toward your hairline and keep it directly *on* your cheekbones, not underneath.

STEPPIN' OUT: THE DAZZLE LOOK

A special occasion calls for a special face. How much extra nighttime dazzle you apply to your face (and body, too) depends on the occasion. A sit-down dinner party does not call for the extravagant glamour that an exciting evening of dancing at a party or a discotheque does. For important nights on the town, you will want to remove your daytime makeup, soak in a luxurious bath, indulge in a Nightbird Facial (see Chapter 1, page 41), and then apply the intense and sparkling makeup that will give your face fascination.

Because the soft glow of night lighting tends to fade cosmetics and make their colors less intense, you will want to wear deeper shades at night. Don't overdo. Makeup should always be carefully applied and blended onto your skin, no matter how dramatic the shades you use. Remember to apply your cosmetics under natural daytime bulbs. You want to look like an extra-special version of your usual self, not a candidate for the circus. Below are some of my special tips.

HERITAGE SECRETS

Special Makeup From Africa

Women in tribes all over Africa are famous for decorating their faces with unique designs. (Among the Fula, a nomadic tribe between Senegal and Chad, the *men* are the experts, wearing some of the most elegant makeup in the world, including a yellow-toned foundation and a dark-blue lipstick.) Designing your face with tribal-type markings is not the least bit primitive but especially unusual and chic (a lot of trend-setters in Los Angeles are doing it). Applying African-style makeup will give you a chance to use your cosmetics in a different way and put your artistic instincts to work. For a basic tribal design, try:

1. Coloring your lids heavily with a dark-green or navy-blue pencil. Extend the shadow beyond the corner in a neat and distinct triangular shape.

2. Adding diagonal black lines that extend down from the lower lid of your eye to the top of your cheeks with a well-sharpened pencil.

3. Drawing narrow black lines across the bridge of your nose.

You can experiment using other colors and shapes on your cheeks, nose, and eyes. Make sure you perfect your technique before you take your new makeup out of doors, and wear an exotic outfit that will complement your makeup style.

1. Dazzle Foundation

Apply a foundation one shade deeper than the one you use during the day. The deeper tone should still match your basic skin tones, and only subtly intensify them.

2. Dazzle Contouring

Contour shading, too, can be deeper in color than your daytime cream. Apply as I instructed in The Complete Makeup. You can also add a line of contouring directly beneath your cheekbone (where you place your cream rouge) and blend it out carefully toward your ears. This extra touch will emphasize your cheekbones and give you sexy hollows beneath them.

3. Dazzle Rouge

Your cream rouge color will also be deeper for evening. Try a dramatic brick tone. Blend it in but make sure the color really registers.

4. Dazzle Powder

Apply powder as usual—not more!

5. Dazzle Eyes

For special evenings your eyes can be dramatized in exciting ways. Now is the time to put on your silvers, platinums, golds, bronzes, sparkling blues, and burgundies, or your pearlized pencils and shadows—any color that shines and reflects light is right for evening wear. Line your eyes with a pencil as usual— above the lashes on the upper lid and below the lashes on the lower lid—but add more liner to the lower lid and smudge it a bit farther down below the eyes so it makes a definite impression. Bring the selected shadow to the outer corner of your eye and smudge it out beyond the corner. You can also highlight the eyebone with a sparkling shadow or even a glittery mica powder. Remember, nighttime lighting washes red undertones out of eye shadows. So avoid soft plum shades and wear more vivid colors or pearlized sparklers that catch the light.

6. Dazzle Lashes

False lashes provide a mysterious and dramatic frame for nighttime eyes. Today lashes should not be too long or too full. Put the strip of artificial lash on your eyelid to get an idea of how long it should be to still look natural, then remove it and trim it to the desired length with nail scissors.

Putting Lashes On

First, place a good-sized hand mirror flat on your dressing table. Squeeze a little of the special cosmetic glue on a tissue, and take a toothpick and run it over the glue. Then, holding the lash with the band toward you, run the toothpick over the band. Bend over so you are looking down into the mirror. Your eyelid will be semiclosed in this position, which makes it easier to apply the lash. Using your forefinger and thumb, press the lash down as close to your own lashline as possible. Press the band with your finger from the inner corner to the outer corner of your eye. You may want to add a light coat of mascara to the lashes after they are on securely.

A Word About Glue

Many glues sting and irritate the eye, depending on your sensitivity to the ingredients. If one glue bothers you, abandon it and try another. Eventually you will find one that works. Remember to pull the glue off the band of the lashes every time you remove them. Like everything else that goes near the eye, it is important to keep the false lashes clean. There is a special solution you can buy to bathe them in.

7. Dazzle Lip Color

Outline your lips more distinctly for evening in a brighter or deeper shade of lip-lining pencil. Nighttime is when the pearlized lipstick shades look their best. Use a darker shade or a shiny, glowing one. You can also apply a pearlized shade over a dark one for an intensified gleam.

8. Dazzle Blush

For evening apply blush to the parts of your face you highlight for daytime wear, but choose a more intense shade—like a brick tone or a deep burgundy. You can also use a sparkling blush. Try adding blush to your earlobes and to the cleft of your chin.

9. Extra Dazzle Touches for the Body and Face

Glitter

Many cosmetic companies make shimmering mica powders in rainbow shades, which you can apply to many places on your body and face. Our dark skin makes a fabulous palette for these shiny glitters. If your skin is dark, try copper, bronze, fuchsia, or blue shades. If you have a lighter complexion, try the silvers, pinks, golds, and greens. Put the glitter on the backs of your hands, on your collarbones and shoulders, and on the part of your leg that flashes from the slit in an evening dress. I touch my lips and eyebones with these glittery powders, too. Even the mature woman can wear a conservative touch of glitter on her collarbones.

HERITAGE SECRETS

Sexy Egyptian Body Glitter

Egyptian beauties were the first to use body glitter, gilding their nipples with an elegant gold frost. When you are entertaining a special someone, you might try using a gold or bronze mica powder on this super-sexy part of you, for a special under-negligée surprise. Gold or bronze mica powder in your cleavage is also a guaranteed gaze catcher for glamorous evenings.

Hairline Color

If you wear your hair slicked back into a fashionable knot or in an upswept style, try brushing some color into your hairline. Loosen some of the powder from a container of powdered eye shadow with a nail file and brush the color into your hair, starting at the hairline, with a medium-sized makeup brush or fine-toothed comb. You can also use a glittery mica powder. Blues, magentas, turquoises, silvers, or golds are the best shades for our dark hair. Make sure you don't get any excess powder on your face.

Beauty Marks

I've always thought beauty marks were glamorous in an old-fashioned Hollywood style. I hated to lose a fine specimen I had on my cheek to the dermatologist, who recommended it be removed. For special occasions I put it back on with an eyebrow pencil. Try adding fake beauty marks to your shoulder, cheek-bone, or the corner of your mouth. You may want to use a sequin, applied with a touch of eyelash glue, for a beauty mark. I also like to darken the cleft of my chin with an eyebrow pencil or a colored eye pencil to emphasize this sexy indentation.

REDESIGNING YOUR FACE

Almost no woman is completely satisfied with the face nature gave her. Most of us look at ourselves in the mirror and see the nose, the lips, the eyes we wish were a little different. Ironically, those very noses, eyes, and lips are often the features the friends and relatives closest to us admire or love. Fifteen years ago I had what everyone thought was the perfect nose. I hated it myself. I knew it was a turned-up nose, and I knew other people could see my nostrils as clearly as anything else on my face. Everyone said, "Please don't have your nose done!" Once I was at the studio signing a contract, and the director said, "Whatever else you do, don't touch your nose." Finally, I could no longer live with that nose everyone else adored. I looked in the mirror and said, "*I* do not want a turned-up nose," and I went to a plastic surgeon and had it transformed into a longer, more elegant one. Only Barbara made that decision, and I still believe it was the right decision for me.

The worst thing you can do to yourself is tear your face apart. It is important not to obsess about flaws, because if you overfocus on a part of your face you don't like, it can prevent you from seeing (and working with) the pretty parts, and it can give you an inferiority complex that will reduce your self-confidence. On the other hand, if some part of your face really bothers you, you have the privilege and the right to try your best to change it. Plastic surgery can now do wonders to change features and alter the effects of aging. A complete face-lift will take years off you, and a complex operation called blepharoplasty will dissolve some of the creases and folds that age causes around the eyes. A good plastic surgeon can change the shape of your nose, your ears, your chin, and your jaw, provided you are willing to contribute one very important ingredient—money! Many of the features you dislike can be redesigned by skillful application of cosmetics. Below are my secrets for changing troublesome areas in your face.

Covering Flaws in the Skin

1. Concealing Light Patches

Some black people suffer from a skin disease called *vitiglio*, which leaves pink or lightened patches in their dark complexions. If this is your problem, take a dark contour-shading cream and apply it to the too-light areas, filling in those areas only. Blend carefully at the edges so the dark contouring fades naturally into the normal-colored areas. Then take the regular foundation that matches your skin tone and apply it over the contour shading and to the rest of your face. This is the best way I know to cover these imperfections without using a heavy, unnatural foundation.

2. Concealing Dark Patches

If your skin has dark discolorations, take a foundation that is two shades lighter than your regular base and apply it directly to the darkened areas, blending carefully. Then put your regular foundation over the dark areas and apply to the rest of your face.

3. Concealing Occasional Blemishes

Almost everybody has experienced the agony of sprouting a large, disfiguring pimple just before an important occasion. When this happens to my models before a television show, I use an eyebrow or eye pencil to transform the pimple into a dramatic beauty spot. The pencil won't irritate the pimple, provided you make sure to clean your face properly later. You can also conceal blemished areas by patting extra foundation over them after you've applied a thin layer to your entire face as you usually do. A little extra powder will also help disguise the problem area. Remember, the best cure for blemishes is careful treatment and cleansing.

Improving the Shape of Your Face

In Step 2 of The Complete Makeup (Contour Shading), I suggested methods to make your face seem closer to a perfect oval. You can also use cream rouge to give the illusion of an oval face.

If your face is too round . . . Round, full cheeks have a sensuous loveliness, but if you want to make your face seem slimmer, do not apply rouge to your cheekbones. Instead, apply it in a triangular shape directly beneath your eyes. The point of the triangle should point down. This will bring the attention of the eye to the center of your face. Another technique for contouring a round face is to put a pencil at the end of your eyebrow so that it falls straight down toward your cheek. Start your cream rouge (you can also use powder blush here) at the outside edge of the pencil and blend it toward your temple. This pulls the focus of attention away from the round, center part of your face.

If your face is too long . . . Use your cream rouge to create a rectangular shape that begins below the center of your eye and travels over your cheekbone. Blend the rouge up and around to your temple. Then add a square-shaped patch of powder blush to your forehead. These techniques should help round out your face.

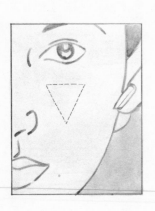

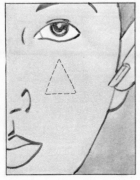

If your face is too square jawed or heart shaped . . . After you've blended your contouring cream onto the jaw area, create a triangle shape below the center of your eye with your cream rouge. The point of the triangle should point up toward your eye. This will help soften your face's angular planes.

Improving the Shape of Your Lips

1. Minimizing the size of your lips

Many black women feel their lips are too large, and try to make them look smaller by applying lipstick only to the center of their lips. This technique is not effective. If you want to minimize your lips, apply foundation to your mouth, masking out the area you feel is too large, and filling in the area you want to emphasize with lipstick, using a brush. You can also use a pencil to draw a new outline, inside the natural outlines of your lips, before you apply the lipstick.

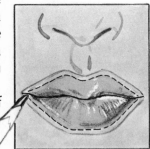

You can use the same technique on your bottom lip only if you feel it is too large.

2. Unevenly shaped lips

To perfect the shape of uneven lips, simply use a lip lining pencil to add to the part of your lip you feel is too small. Draw a new outline for the smaller area just above your lip's natural outline. If you are not sure which part of your mouth needs correction, try blotting your lips when you're wearing lipstick on a piece of plain white paper. This will give you an image of your lip shape that you can examine. Try improving this "lip drawing" with a pencil before you begin to work on your real mouth.

Perfecting the Shape of Your Eyes

Before you consider redesigning the shape or size of your eyes, remember that they, more than any feature, express the individual you. Unusual eyes, which do not conform to an abstract or ideal standard of beauty, are often the feature that most impresses other people. The techniques below will actually help you reveal the special beauty of unusual eyes.

1. Protruding Eyes

You will want to make the protruding part of your eye appear to recede by selecting a very dark blue-gray or smoky-colored shadow and applying it directly to the part of the lid that bulges out. Blend, then apply a deep burgundy or brown shadow to the crease. Finally, highlight the bone beneath the brow with a very light lavender or dusty pink shadow.

2. Deep-set Eyes

If you want to bring deep-set eyes forward, use a light shade of shadow on the lid and blend it up above the crease. Pale greens, blues, violets, silvers, and plums are most effective. I usually use only one pale color on deep-set eyes, but you can blend two shades together. The less shadow you pile on the lid, the more the eye itself is revealed. Finally, I use a darker shade just beneath the brow on the eyebone. If you want to use eye liner, use it only on the upper lid from the center of the eye to the outer corner. Make sure the line is thin and close to the lashes.

3. Small Eyes

To enlarge small eyes, stay away from dark liners. Remember, when you frame a picture it always looks smaller. If you want to use a liner, select a light, pretty shade and make sure the line is thin and close to the base of the lashes. Begin the line from the center of the eye and extend it to the outer corner. Use only a touch of the palest liner below the lower fringe of lashes. On the upper lid, use a light shade of eye shadow to the crease and blend a darker shade in the crease and up past it, blending it out toward the corner of the eye.

4. Close-set Eyes

To give the illusion that close-set eyes are set wider apart, never put liner in the corner of the eye close to the nose. Start the line one third of the way in toward the pupil of the eye, on both the upper and lower lids. Select a pale shade of eye shadow for the inside corner of the eye, and a darker shade for the center of the lid. Bring the darker shade out beyond the corner of the eye. Blend the pale and dark shades together. Make sure to tweeze your eyebrows so they don't grow together. Apply mascara only to lashes at the outer corner of the eye.

1 & 2: *The Complete Makeover*: The model's natural "no makeup look" was transformed by The Complete Makeup and a new hairstyle. Cream rouge and contouring emphasize her beautiful cheekbones, and a smoky shadow adds sultry drama to her eyes. Her hair was cut in a bowl shape, blown out and straightened with a beveling iron (a flatter, wider version of a curling iron).

1

2

3

4

3 & 4: *The Complete Makeover*: The model's skin was evened out with a foundation that reveals its undertones, and her face was contoured for a slim, high-fashion look. Her lipstick emphasizes the beauty of full lips. Her hair was styled to give an illusion of length to her round face.

5 & 6: *Wrong to right*: In photo 5 the model is wearing the wrong makeup. She has tried to lighten her complexion with a pale shade of foundation. The result: an unattractive ashy tone. She has applied a bright blue shadow to the eye bone and extended her black liner beyond the corners of her eyes (both no-nos). Her brows are too dark and harsh, and her hairstyle is too severe for her face. In 6 the right shade of foundation and makeup, applied with the techniques described in "The Complete Makeup," creates an elegant beauty. Her hair was pressed and set, then styled in a chignon with a soft wave in front.

5

6

7

8

7 & 8: *Beauty knows no number*: The model is a senior citizen. In 7 she is wearing no makeup at all. In 8 she demonstrates how The Complete Makeup softens flaws and glamorizes the mature face.

9 & 10: *The Dazzle Look*: In 9 the model is wearing The Complete Makeup, a sophisticated daytime look. For evening she has applied a more intense shade of lipstick and rouge and emphasized her eyes with glittery shadows and false lashes. The difference is subtle but dramatic.

9

10

Styles in photos 1-6 were created by the B. J. Bubbles Salon. Makeup is by Barbara Walden and staff.

1. *The long curly perm:* The model's tight, natural curl was stretched and lengthened by a reverse perm process for a longer look with more volume. The wash-and-wear style was naturally dried.

2. The model's shoulder-length hair was moistened with a gel, then rolled on the sides and top for a soft, modern cornrow effect. Hair was braided in the back. This sophisticated style is suitable for both business and evening wear and can be done with short or long hair.

3. *Blow-dry and curl:* The model's hair was precision cut to frame her face, then blown out with a dryer and curled with a curling iron.

4. The model's short, curly perm was combed back on the sides and forward in the front into a spiral curl, then glamorized with two rhinestone barrettes. A short cut in any texture can be styled and dressed up for evening with pretty ornaments.

5. For a long, braided look, artificial extensions were braided into the model's own hair, which is three inches long. Gold thread was wound around the braids in front.

Styles were created by Barbara Morris, Denise Clark, and Rubin Ellison of the B. J. Bubbles Salon in New York.

1 & 2: *The Complete Makeover:* The model's natural "no makeup look" was transformed by The Complete Makeup and a new hairstyle. Cream rouge and contouring emphasize her beautiful cheekbones, and a smoky shadow adds sultry drama to her eyes. Her hair was cut in a bowl shape, blown out and straightened with a beveling iron (a flatter, wider version of a curling iron).

1

2

3

4

3 & 4: *The Complete Makeover:* The model's skin was evened out with a foundation that reveals its undertones, and her face was contoured for a slim, high-fashion look. Her lipstick emphasizes the beauty of full lips. Her hair was styled to give an illusion of length to her round face.

5 & 6: *Wrong to right:* In photo 5 the model is wearing the wrong makeup. She has tried to lighten her complexion with a pale shade of foundation. The result: an unattractive ashy tone. She has applied a bright blue shadow to the eye bone and extended her black liner beyond the corners of her eyes (both no-nos). Her brows are too dark and harsh, and her hairstyle is too severe for her face. In 6 the right shade of foundation and makeup, applied with the techniques described in "The Complete Makeup," creates an elegant beauty. Her hair was pressed and set, then styled in a chignon with a soft wave in front.

5   6

7 & 8: *Beauty knows no number:* The model is a senior citizen. In 7 she is wearing no makeup at all. In 8 she demonstrates how The Complete Makeup softens flaws and glamorizes the mature face.

7   8

9 & 10: *The Dazzle Look:* In 9 the model is wearing The Complete Makeup, a sophisticated daytime look. For evening she has applied a more intense shade of lipstick and rouge and emphasized her eyes with glittery shadows and false lashes. The difference is subtle but dramatic.

9   **10**

Styles in photos 1-6 were created by the B. J. Bubbles Salon. Makeup is by Barbara Walden and staff.

1. *The long curly perm*: The model's tight, natural curl was stretched and lengthened by a reverse perm process for a longer look with more volume. The wash-and-wear style was naturally dried.

2. The model's shoulder-length hair was moistened with a gel, then rolled on the sides and top for a soft, modern cornrow effect. Hair was braided in the back. This sophisticated style is suitable for both business and evening wear and can be done with short or long hair.

3. *Blow-dry and curl*: The model's hair was precision cut to frame her face, then blown out with a dryer and curled with a curling iron.

4. The model's short, curly perm was combed back on the sides and forward in the front into a spiral curl, then glamorized with two rhinestone barrettes. A short cut in any texture can be styled and dressed up for evening with pretty ornaments.

5. For a long, braided look, artificial extensions were braided into the model's own hair, which is three inches long. Gold thread was wound around the braids in front.

Styles were created by Barbara Morris, Denise Clark, and Rubin Ellison of the B. J. Bubbles Salon in New York.

5. Wide-set Eyes

Wide-set eyes are an asset, and few women complain about them. To modify the wide-set look, start your liner from the very inner corner of the eye, on both the top and bottom lids. The liner on the top should meet the liner on the bottom, almost in a circle. This draws your eyes together. Your shadow, too, should start at the inmost corner of the eye and fade out as it moves toward the outer corner. The lashes that are closest to your nose should be emphasized with mascara.

6. Flat Eyes

If your eyes seem too flat and don't have curved contours, you can improve their shape by first applying a fairly dark color of eye shadow to the outer third of your lid, closest to the corner of your eye, and to the inner third, closest to your nose. Then add a pale or shimmery color to the center of your lid and blend it slightly.

7. Disguising Heavy Folds

If your lids are weighted by heavy folds, put a dark, smoky-colored shadow directly on the fold itself, and blend it up and out toward the end of your eyebrow. Use a light shadow beneath the brow and line the eyes only from the center of the lid to the outer corner.

3

Creating Good Hair

WE HAVE BEAUTIFUL HAIR

Our hair, like our dark skin and strong features, is an important part of our special beauty. Its interesting textures range from kinky to wavy to perfectly straight. Like our skin, our dark hair contains exciting undertones of color—subtle browns, rusts, mahoganies, and blues—glowing with deep glints of refracted light. Beauticians say black hair is easy to style. Comb it, roll it, pin it up or back with ornaments, or twist it into braids—we can do anything with our hair and it stays—giving us a choice of high-fashion, dramatic hairstyles that are fun to create and simple to change.

GOOD HAIR VS. BAD HAIR

For centuries we believed that a few of us had "good hair" and most of us had "bad hair." Good hair, we thought, was wavy hair with a silky texture that blew in the wind, like white people's did, and bad hair was kinky, "nappy" hair. Those of us who had "bad hair" did everything in our power to make it "good." In the old days we wouldn't be caught dead in public without our hair painstakingly pressed and curled. We didn't straighten it out of choice, but out of some inner self-criticism we called "necessity."

I remember envying my mother and sisters, who had beautiful, long, almost straight hair. I thought I was unfortunate to have
inherited my father's strong but kinky hair, and soon became a
virtual slave to my hot comb and rollers. When I went to
Hollywood I refused to try out for a part unless my hair was
"done," and then the doing took hours. When my agent called
me to come for an interview on short notice, I had to decline
because there wasn't time to press my hair, set it, and wait for the
curl to take hold. He thought I was being temperamental. Once,
to prove my point, I jumped in a cab with my hair exactly the way
it looked when I got up in the morning—puffed out into a kinky
natural—just to show him what it was like when it wasn't pressed
and curled. He was convinced. In those days, before black was
beautiful, any kind of natural was *out*. Later on in the sixties,
ironically enough, I was criticized for not wearing an Afro style.

FREEDOM TO CHOOSE

Today there are many style solutions for the black woman's hair.
There are no "musts" or "have to's." We feel spiritually free to
wear our hair the way we like—in natural styles which reveal the
personality of its kink and curl, chemically permed, or temporarily
relaxed. I still prefer to wear my hair pressed and curled (an Afro
or braids are just not made for my face, and I'm highly allergic to
chemical relaxers); but a styling gel I invented to solve my hair
problem and those of my customers helps me set my hair in
minutes instead of hours. Though the slightest bit of humidity
makes my hair revert, I can now say, "Let it be!" instead of
rushing back to my dressing table to do it again. Today I choose
the style I want because I want it, not because some dictating
voice, inside or outside my head, says it's right. I now know that
"good" hair means strong, healthy hair styled in a way that
appeals to *Barbara,* and bad hair is part of the past.

TIMES ARE CHANGING

In the past many of us styled our hair at home, using time-honored
techniques taught us by relatives and friends. If someone in our
neighborhood knew how to "do hair," her house became a
popular meeting place, where we gathered to experiment with

new styles and skills. It gave us a warm and intimate feeling to work on each other's heads like that, and it brought us closer together. (Fortunately, this fine custom hasn't disappeared; we still need each other for cornrows and braids.) When we wanted to visit a salon, however, there were few places to go. The beauty parlors that catered to us black women were not equipped to deal with all of us who needed professional hair care. Sometimes it took almost all day to get our hair relaxed or pressed and curled. The beautician might shampoo our hair (making it revert, of course), then stick us in a long line to wait our turn for the vital finishing touches. Sometimes that turn didn't come until two in the afternoon, and we were prisoners in the salon because we couldn't leave until our natural heads were redesigned.

In those days there was virtually no education for the black-oriented beautician. The cosmetology schools devoted only a fraction of training time to teaching students about our hair; the few experts available learned mainly on the job, through trial and error. Unfortunately, this is still largely the case. Though our rising economic status has caused some major salon chains, devoted especially to our needs, to mushroom across the country, and large cities have excellent stylists specializing in black hair, there are not enough professionals to give black hair the attention it needs, especially in nonurban areas. For this reason every black woman owes it to herself to get a thorough hair education—to learn as much as possible about how to handle her hair and how to ask for, and get, what she wants when she goes to the salon.

OUR HAIR IS DELICATE

Believe it or not, 90 percent of black people have thin, flyaway hair. Our hair looks thick and strong, but it's strictly an illusion. Though we have almost double the number of hairs on our head as white or Asian people (an average of 500,000 hairs per capita), each individual hair is thin and fragile and breaks as easily as a delicate thread, even in normal brushing and combing. Needless to say, few of us stop at brushing and combing. We subject our fine hair to an incredible variety of harsh processes: Pressing combs, curling irons, driers, and rollers are all extra hard on our tender hair, and chemicals, like dyes and relaxers, truly threaten it.

Many of us have had the devastating experience of experimenting with some special concoction to get a new texture or style and found ourselves with frazzled, breaking hair that looked terrible and kept us miserable for months afterward. (I nearly poisoned myself when the chemicals from a relaxer entered my bloodstream.) Experts say that black hair breaks when subjected to only half the amount of chemicals straight-haired people can stand. Yet who buys and uses a huge number of the chemicals on the market? We do! As a result, beauticians say we are ruining our hair; we no longer have the thick, luxuriant hair our mothers and grandmothers had, and this, to my mind, is a national tragedy. Because I believe that no style can possibly be any more beautiful than the quality of hair involved, the following pages will be filled with "Never-Nevers" and warnings—perhaps more than you want to hear. These negative precautions, however, should help you get the style you want without the breakage and damage that destroy your hair and peace of mind.

Finding a "Doctor" for Your Hair

Your hair is your crowning glory and deserves the same special attention as any other part of you. We all let a dentist work on our teeth and a doctor take care of our body; we should also let skilled professionals care for our hair. Finding a first-rate stylist you can trust can be just as difficult as finding a good doctor, and calls for some careful investigation.

Selecting a Salon

Step 1: If you see another woman (friend or stranger) with a beautiful, healthy, well-styled head of hair, don't hesitate to ask her where she has it done and which operator at the salon does it.

Step 2: Check out the salon with a go-see visit. You might feel strange lurking around like a CIA spy, so stop in for a manicure or pedicure. While you are there, keep your eyes and ears open. Notice how the women who've had their hair styled look when they leave. Do they seem formal and uneasy with the stylist, or is the rapport warm and friendly? Observe the different stylists and how they work. Don't let the elite or pleasant atmosphere of the salon make your decision for you.

Step 3: If you like what you see, have a preliminary chat with the manager. Discuss fees. If you plan to have your hair permed or colored, find out not only how much the initial transformation will cost, but how much you should expect to spend on retouches, and how often you will need them. Don't forget to include tips in your calculations. If you're satisfied, make an appointment.

Getting Ready for Your First Appointment

When you visit a new salon, you should bring a well-considered idea of what you want done to your hair. If you know you want a change but you don't know what kind, peruse the hair and fashion magazines for black women. If you see an appealing style, look in the mirror, hold the picture beside your face, and actively try to imagine it with your own face shape and hair type. Try to pin or comb your own hair into an approximation of the style. Look at other women in the street; observe how they wear their hair. Which styles are most effective and why?

Once you have a styling idea, ask yourself if it's realistic. Beauticians say the most difficult client is the confused lady who comes into the salon trailing four inches of hair and demands a style that requires twelve. Be honest with yourself when you appraise the length, texture, and condition of your hair. Don't set your heart on any one style. Remember, you're going to the salon to take advantage of a professional's expertise. Your crowning glory will probably be a compromise of your wildest dreams, the stylist's artistic imagination, and the possibilities your individual head of hair has to offer.

Talk to Your Stylist

Many ladies are intimidated by beauticians, just as they are intimidated by doctors. They either accept whatever the stylist tells them, or fail to ask enough questions when they don't. Your stylist is—or should be—a real human being with a voice and ears. The most important part of your first salon visit is to establish a working communication with him or her. There are some arrogant prima donnas who will give you a fabulous style, but, in general, a good stylist is a sympathetic, down-to-earth person who wants to hear your ideas and tell you hers (or his). Talk freely to the stylist about your hair problems, and discuss the style you

have in mind. She (or he) may tell you why it won't work with
your hair type or face shape. The stylist may tell you the style calls
for a chemical process your hair won't withstand and may suggest
a modified version of it. In any case, the stylist should be able to
describe the style she wants to create and tell you why it will work
with your face, body type, and hair type, as well as give you a
thorough analysis of the texture and condition of your hair. Your
job is to quiz and question until the specifics are clear in your
mind. If you don't know what the stylist is talking about, ask to see
a picture of the style.

Your stylist should inspire a feeling of confidence and
security. If she or he seems anxious to get the job over with as
quickly as possible, collect your money and send you home, if
she or he makes you feel like an unattractive worm instead of a
gorgeous lady, if she or he is evasive or noncommittal and tells
you to "relax" or "not worry" when you ask questions, you've
come to the wrong place. Pack up your pocketbook and go home,
or resolve to look for a new salon as soon as your first
appointment is over.

Never-Never Number One

Never lie to your stylist or withhold information about what
you have already done to your hair—however foolish or drastic. If
you are contemplating a chemical service like perming or dyeing,
be sure to tell the stylist everything (and I mean *everything)* you
have used on your hair in the past year, including dyes, home
relaxers, and heat processes. Describe the results and any
problems you've had. If she doesn't ask, tell her anyway. The
stylist can only make an intelligent decision about what product to
use on your hair, and how to use it, when she learns this all-
important data.

Communicating Your Personal Style

Always go to the salon wearing the clothes and makeup you
usually wear—the "look" you want your hairstyle to match. A
good stylist will pick up your vibrations, but you have to give her
some help. Tell her how you see yourself and give her some
important facts about your life-style, including how much time
and money you have to invest in your hair. If you spend most of

your time in business outfits, you will not want to combine them with hanging braids decorated with conch shells. If you are a free spirit, who rarely wears much makeup and always wears loose clothes or jeans, a very sophisticated short cut will make you feel like an imposter. If your life is varied (office days and romantic evenings), ask for a hairstyle you can modify and dress up or down, and find out exactly how to do it. Remember, the style can't wear you, you have to wear the style.

Enjoying Changes

Most of us change and grow every year and want our outer selves to reflect the new woman inside. Nevertheless, many ladies hesitate to change their hair more than any other aspect of their appearance. *Change* is a threatening word when it is applied to hair, and we often opt for the same antiquated look long after we've outgrown it because we simply can't envision something new or the effect it will have on our lives. "What if my husband hates it?" we ask ourselves. "What if it looks terrible?" Fortunately, no change of hairstyle can be a total disaster for long. Hair, unlike the other organs of your body, grows back the way it was, no matter what you do to it. Often a new style may not look the way you imagined, and it will take your mind (and your hair) some time to adjust. Hair does go into "shock" right after it's been cut and may look much better a few days or a week later. It may take time to learn to manage a permed style. Compliments from friends and the men in your life will soon tell you if your new style reflects the real you. If you're unhappy with the style or if your hair shows signs of damage, don't hesitate to return to the salon. A reputable stylist will be only too glad to do what she can to satisfy you—at no extra cost.

Never-Never Number Two

Never contemplate a new style when you are totally depressed. A new style will never work for you at a miserable time, because the lift you need is far greater than your hair, in any shape or form, can give you. You are bound to have unrealistic expectations and be disappointed with what you get. Rash decisions to home-perm or dye, too, are most often made when you're feeling down.

Get an Education

When you visit a salon, you're paying for hair education as well as a new style. Take advantage of the golden opportunity. Keep your eyes open and watch carefully what the stylist does. Ask questions about each procedure. Notice what shampoos and conditioners she uses on your hair and ask why she has selected those products. If you are getting your hair permed or colored, get as much information as possible about the type of products used and the application process. This will be valuable if you travel or move and have to change salons.

You shouldn't leave the salon without knowing what to do with your hair at home. Ignorance is not bliss. Ask how the style should be washed, dried, and combed, and how it can be changed for more dramatic, nighttime looks. Try the combing, blow-drying, or pinning process yourself before you leave, if possible, and ask the stylist to watch and guide you. At first, a new style may need salon upkeep, but eventually you should be able to handle it yourself, keeping your hair-care bills to a minimum.

Styling Vacation

If you live in a nonurban area, a trip to a large city may give you a chance to take advantage of the stars of the styling world. Notice who designs the styles featured in your favorite magazine. If he or she has a salon in your vacation city, make an appointment. If you have a relative or friend in that city, you can ask her to recommend a reputable salon. The style you choose should not demand elaborate upkeep and retouches your local salon can't do. Make sure you get all the specifics on home care. Be secretive: Don't tell the stylist you're from out of town. If the stylist knows you aren't returning, he or she may not be inclined to get too involved and give you the special attention you came for.

Style Guidelines

Below are some basic guidelines to help you make an informed decision about how to style your hair.

Face Shape

The shape of your face, its contours and bone structure, is an important consideration. Your hairstyle should emphasize your most attractive features and steer the eye away from imperfections. Though few of us have totally round, long, square, heart-shaped, or oval faces, all our faces *tend* toward one shape or another. The sketch you made to help yourself apply makeup should tell you which shape belongs to you. The prescriptions below can be modified, of course, depending how long, round, square, oval or heart-shaped your face really is.

If you have a round face . . . your hair should be cut so it falls away from the face and lies flat on the sides. A style that gives you height at the top of your head, length at the nape of your neck, and reveals your ears will be flattering. A lot of hair puffing around your cheeks will only make your face look rounder.

If your face is long . . . with a long chin, it needs to have its angular lines softened by hair around the face. A good cut will balance the weight of the hair at the cheeks, the nape of the neck, and the jawline. Your hair should *not* be cut high on the sides and left long in the back. Chignons, pulled severely back from the face, will also emphasize the long lines of your chin. If you want to wear a chignon, let tendrils and curls escape the knot to form a frame around the face.

If your face is square-jawed . . . or has a heavy look at the jawline, your style should not emphasize the jaw area. Your hair should be cut away from the face, though not as much as if your face is very round. You can carry some hair around the face, but not a billowing mass. Your hair will look most attractive cut to a length just above the jawline. A stylist can also contour it in an attractive sweep which falls to the jaw.

If your face is oval or heart-shaped . . . you have the ideal shape for most styles, and most will be attractive, provided they also enhance your figure, the length of your neck, and match your overall look.

Length of Neck

If your neck is short . . . avoid wearing your hair long—one length cascading to your shoulders. A stylist can cut your hair in angles which reveal the neck and give the illusion that it's longer.

If your neck is long . . . a swan's neck is a beautiful attribute, but your hairstyle should soften this extended line. Curly hair around the neck will reveal its beauty, without making it seem too long or thin.

Your Figure

If you are heavy . . . the right hairstyle can take ten pounds off your weight. Your face will probably be too round if you're on the heavy side. If this is the case, hair should be cut away from the face to reveal your beautiful eyes, mouth, or cheekbones. The hair should also be tapered toward the back, giving it length, which will prevent your head from looking too small for your body.

If you are tall and slender . . . you can wear most styles, but you'll want to avoid a severe or dramatic look that will make your face and figure seem angular or stern. Tendrils on the forehead, around the face and neck, or long hair, cut just a little higher than shoulder level, will certainly become you. Volume or fullness in the style, as in a curly, tousled look, will soften your face and figure, too.

If you are petite . . . you'll want to avoid overpowering styles that make your head look off-balance with the rest of your body. If you are tiny and thin, a close-cut pixie or Afro style is ideal, as is a neat chignon worn close to the head. You can wear dramatic styles, provided they are scaled down to fit you. Avoid big, fluffy Afros; they make a small lady look about to topple over.

The Precision Cut

A good haircut is an essential element of hairstyle. Until recently, the black woman went to the salon primarily to get her hair "done"—shampooed, relaxed, and curled. Because our hair tended to break off all by itself, we thought, "Why cut it?" Black beauticians from the old school were indoctrinated to cut hair seldom, if ever.

Today, as we tend toward styles that need less maintenance, a modern precision cut is a necessity. Simply defined, a precision cut is one in which every snip of the stylist's scissors is intended to have a specific effect and make the hair fall in a specific direction. Much training and talent go into a precision cut, and not every stylist has them. How do you know if your cut is a good one?

• A precision cut puts a line or style into the hair, enabling it to fall into a definite shape or form even before you set it or blow it dry.

• The ends of a good haircut blend evenly and don't stick out every which way.

• A precision-cut head of hair will have bounce and movement and hold a set well.

Cutting Damaged Hair

If your hair is damaged, broken, or torn, grit your teeth and cut it off. The long hair you treasure isn't really long if the last four inches of it are limp, porous, or split. Minus the dead weight, your hair will be easier to set and care for. Damaged hair is never very attractive because it lacks vitality and movement.

If you've ruined your hair with a chemical, the quickest way to get healthy hair again is to cut away the damaged parts down to the point where the breakage stops and new virgin hair begins. If this point is too close to the scalp, the stylist will trim the damaged hair in stages in the course of several visits to the salon. As your hair is growing in, she will try to blend your good new hair with the old damaged hair using precision techniques.

Cutting to Condition

A regular trim should be part of your hair-conditioning regimen. Trimming hair that shows signs of damage is the best way to prevent that damage from continuing up the hair shaft and devastating the entire hair. Once an end is split, the splitting process will spread until stopped by scissors. No deep-conditioning treatment, I'm sorry to say, will miraculously restore broken or torn hair.

You may go to the salon to have your split ends snipped and emerge with what seems to you a "short" haircut, and rage toward the stylist who dared shear your precious locks. This misunderstanding occurs because she or he observed that the broken ends were not smack-dab at the bottom of your hair, but scattered throughout. When she cut away all the damage, she also cut away a lot of your hair. A competent stylist will leave some length on the bottom and clean out damaged hair at the top. The result: shorter hair with more volume.

Never-Never Number Three

Never cut your hair at home. Though it's human nature to snip stray ends between salon appointments, if you take the scissors to your head with serious intentions to cut and restyle, you're bound to be sorry. To cut hair correctly, you must section it off and cut it in specific directions with specific techniques, modified according to the texture of each head of hair, and according to the direction in which the hair grows. These skills, needless to say, are not developed overnight, but through careful training and experience. Chopping and hacking will leave nasty gaps and recalcitrant ends it will take your beautician several appointments to fix. (And you'll have to listen to her scold you as well; nothing makes a stylist more furious than an ungrateful client who takes matters into her own hands!) Even if you do a passable job, you'll never succeed in cutting the back right or in putting a sophisticated line into your hair.

Growing Long Hair

For generations black women have admired long hair and tried to grow it. My friend Art Dyson, a well-known originator of new styles for black hair, suggests that the reasons we love long hair may be negative. When we first came to the United States as slaves, Art says, our masters required us to cover our heads in their presence. As a result, we came to believe our short, kinky hair was ugly, and envied the white woman's long, smooth mane. Today that envy, still buried in our unconscious minds, makes us continue to want long hair.

Long hair *is* beautiful on some people, but not all of us can, or should, have it. Everyone's hair grows from a quarter to a half inch a month, and everyone's hair grows to a maximum length and no longer. This length is determined by your genetic heritage, which programs your hair to keep growing for a specific number of years and then to stop. Black hair is often prevented from reaching its maximum length by its kinky texture. Kinky hairs grow out of the scalp and wrap around each other; when we pass a comb through them, the comb gets stopped by the natural tangles, and while it doesn't break, the hair does. Lubricating oil from the scalp doesn't flow down the kinky hair shaft as easily either; this causes the ends to dry out and break. Damaging processes, like drying, curling, and perming, also "shorten" our hair by breaking it.

If you want to improve your hair's growing chances, try the following:

• Trim the hair a tiny fraction every six weeks. This will stop the breakage at the ends from traveling up the hair shaft. Eventually your hair, which grows a bit more than you cut, will reach its maximum length.

• Wear a braided style that doesn't require combing until your hair is long.

• Stay away from chemicals, hot driers, rollers, and curling irons. Handle your hair gently when you shampoo and comb. If you press your hair, use an almost-cool hot comb.

• Brush and condition your hair regularly, massage your scalp, and eat a high-protein diet. (See "Basic Hair Care," page 123, for specifics.)

Short Can Be Beautiful

Why shed tears because you can't have what nature denies you? Or weigh down your scalp with a haystack of hair that never really looks good? Consider a short cut if you've tried to grow hair without success. According to Art Dyson, a great believer in the beauty of short hair for the black woman, a chic, modern style can be sculpted to reveal the unique qualities of your head and face, and it is easier to handle, relax, and keep healthy than a long style.

Making the Most of Your Natural Texture

Today we know that *kinky* is a pretty word. Kinks spring out of the scalp with a dynamic excitement that is distinctly black and distinctly you. Kinky hair is not just one texture, but ranges from tight, closely woven kinks, to looser, more wavy kinks, to kinks that grow out of the scalp in ropes or "beads." There are many styles that make these interesting coils work for you. Your naturally textured hair can be worn in an Afro style, scraped back into a chic chignon, or braided in infinite patterns. Natural styles may pose more limitations than relaxed styles, but they are the least affected by weather conditions, like humidity. Below are the pros of some kinky styles, along with information to help you keep them looking their best.

1. The Afro

The Afro, cut close to the head, is one of the easiest styles to care for and the least expensive and time-consuming to maintain. If you have beautiful features and bones, and a head with personality, the Afro will reveal them. The curly Afro that fluffs around the head seems to be going out of style, perhaps because it doesn't mesh with today's sophisticated trends in makeup and fashion, and it tends to overpower the face.

Maintaining the Afro

An Afro style may become dry because sebum secreted by the scalp has to defy gravity to lubricate the ends of the crooked hair shafts. The kinky hairs also wrap around each other and break when you comb. The big, fluffy Afro often requires continuous picking, combing, or setting to give it shape as well as sprays containing drying alcohol—all of which help break the hair. To maintain an in-shape Afro you must:

• Protect your hair from the elements. Wear a scarf or hat in the hot sun or wind, and wear a bathing cap in chlorinated pools or in salt water (both dry the hair). Always wash ocean or pool water out of the hair thoroughly.

• Shampoo less instead of more. Once a week to every ten days should be sufficient if your hair is dry. Use a mild shampoo, and condition your hair regularly, avoiding products that contain alcohol. (See "Basic Hair Care," page 123.)

• Avoid setting a curly Afro with sponge rollers or permanent-waving rods. Use only magnetic or mesh rollers and wrap the ends of the hair with end papers before you set.

• Use a flexible, large-toothed comb with rounded teeth. Metal and wooden picks are hard on the hair.

• Have your Afro trimmed regularly to prevent breakage.

2. Chignons

The chignon is an elegant style that accentuates dramatic cheekbones and eyes. A chignon can be a severe knot, a bun, or a pony tail; you can combine it with braids and decorate it with flowers, barrettes, and other ornaments. A chignon also reveals the pretty tendrils many black women have at the hairline. More than any other style, the chignon makes a rapid transformation from a businesslike to a glamorous evening look. If you don't know how to create an interesting chignon style, invest in a salon appointment and ask the stylist for specific instructions. A chignon should be an economical, do-it-yourself style.

• A chignon should not be so tight that it pulls the hair. A too-tight chignon can cause you to lose hair at the hairline.

• Don't use uncoated rubber bands on the hair; they cause breakage and pull the hair with them when they're removed. Always extract any ornament or tie from the hair gently.

• Trim, condition, massage, and brush your hair regularly, according to the guidelines given in "Basic Hair Care."

3. Braiding

Braiding and cornrowing are part of our African tradition and adapt beautifully to our modern lives. With a little imagination you can create braided styles that are conservative or wildly unique. Developing and trading cornrowing secrets with friends is a good way to cut down on salon costs and put your creative talents to work. Use your sense of style to invent unusual patterns, or do a little library research and copy traditional patterns from books on African tribes. Artificial extensions can be added to your own braids to lengthen them. Remember, some ornamented braided styles are considered too far-out by conservative employers. Unless you're a rebellious soul and don't mind the consequences, design a quiet braided style for business wear.

Braiding also gives damaged hair a rest from chemicals, rollers, driers, hot combs, and even brushing and combing. When your hair is braided, it then can absorb the lubricating sebum that the hair follicles spill out onto the scalp.

Maintaining Braids

Professional braiding costs a fortune, because you are paying for the operator's time. I don't have to tell you that plaiting two hundred braids takes a lot of expensive hours! Even if a friend does your braids, cornrowing is an elaborate, time-consuming process that nobody is anxious to repeat too soon. For this reason you may hesitate to wash your hair often, for fear of disturbing the braids, or to undo the braids in this lifetime.

WASHING BRAIDED HAIR

Braided hair must be washed at least once a week to prevent dirt and bacteria from clogging hair follicles, inhibiting the hair's growth and natural lubrication process. If you wash your hair gently, patting the shampoo on lightly in the shower, you won't disturb the braids. A little cap made out of an old stocking will also protect their formation. Braided styles can be dried naturally; take advantage of this and put away your electric drier for a while.

TAKING OUT THE BRAIDS

Experts say you should remove braids every three weeks. If you have a complicated (or expensive) braided style, you will probably think, "You've got to be kidding!" However strong the temptation, don't leave the braids in forever and a day. Use your judgment, but, remember, every head of hair needs to be brushed and every scalp needs to be stimulated. When you do remove the braids, give your hair a rest for several weeks before you rebraid, and brush, massage, and condition thoroughly. When you first

---

HERITAGE SECRETS

The Universal Beauty of Braids

The cornrows we weave into our hair are a direct gift from our African heritage. In many African tribes the designs made with braids signify a woman's social status. The Cele women in South Africa, for example, braid a girl's hair to notify the world she is of marriageable age. Not only Africans, but women from many cultures have worn their hair in a braided style. Indian women plaited their hair and arranged it in four thin pigtails called *kapardas*, which hung down their back. Etruscan women, too, liked braids. Upper-class wealthy women in ancient Egypt shaved their heads and wore an elaborate wig, braided and dyed ebony black or dark red with henna. Lower-class women imitated them and wore braided wigs, too, but these were made of lowly felt. Later on, Egyptian women plaited their hair in many pigtails— anywhere from eleven to twenty-five, but always an uneven number. Native Americans on this continent, too, have always braided their hair. This beautiful, feminine style has survived for centuries.

remove the braids, separate your hair with your fingers, then wash and condition it before you try to comb it out; this will minimize breakage. In this resting phase you might want to try a chignon, a single pigtail, or combine a few simple braids with your natural curl.

BRAID HAIR SLACKLY

Braids should not create a pulling sensation on the scalp. Very tight braids, worn for too long a time, can place stress on the hair root and create a condition called *traction alopecia,* or bald patches.

REMOVE ORNAMENTS BEFORE YOU SLEEP

Beads and ornaments that bite uncomfortably into your head while resting on a pillow should be removed before you sleep. The painful ornaments can disturb your dreams and dig sores into your scalp. For this reason it's best to choose ornaments that are not braided into the hair.

TAMING BRAIDS

If little hairs sneak out of your braids, tame them with hairspray, then stroke them gently into place with a soft toothbrush. Wearing a silk scarf to bed will also protect the braids while you sleep. A satin pillowcase is easier on braids than a cotton one.

GOING FROM RELAXED BACK TO NATURAL

Hair that has been permed never reverts and becomes kinky again because the chemical permanently destroys the bonds that create the kinky hair configuration. Unfortunately, permed hair that is beginning to grow out is weakest at the point where the chemically treated hair and the virgin regrowth meet—very close to the scalp. Your comb is liable to catch here and pop off the relaxed part of the hair (most of it), or the weight of the relaxed hair alone may be sufficient to cause the strand to break. For this reason it is risky to let the hair remain in two different textures at the same time—both natural and permed.

If your hair has been damaged by a chemical, or if you simply want to try a natural style for a change, the quickest way to make the switch is to cut the relaxed hair off. If you want to make the transition back to natural hair more gradually, you can press the kinky regrowth carefully with a relatively cool hot comb. This will even out the hair's texture and prevent it from breaking at the weak point. Then the old, chemically treated hair can be trimmed an inch or so every month until your new, natural hair completely replaces the perm. You can also braid your hair until you see a significant new growth, then cut off all or most of the permed hair. Because the braided style removes stress from the hair shaft and does not require combing, it is a safe way to wear your two-textured hair.

RELAXING WITH HEAT

Heat straightens the hair temporarily without the damaging effects of chemicals. A press-and-curl style will last until your next shampoo, weather conditions permitting. Another method to temporarily relax the hair, blow-drying and curling, will also give you a straighter, smoother style.

Blow-dry and Curl

If your hair is kinky but relatively silky in texture, you can relax it slightly by blowing it dry, then curling it with curlers or a curling iron. Barbara Morris, a well-known New York stylist, taught me how to do it.

1. Towel dry the excess water out of your hair but leave it fairly wet. Divide the hair into sections—sides, back, top of the head, and bangs (if you have them)—with a wide-toothed comb. Clip the sections you're not working on out of the way with large metal clips.

2. Starting with a side section, lift up a small portion of the hair with a brush toward the top of your head. Hold the drier six inches away from the strand and brush, moving the drier along the strand at the same time. Be sure to keep the drier moving so the heat doesn't scorch one area of your hair. A comb or a brush-type drier will let you eliminate the brush. You are, in effect, drying the underside of your hair first. This gives it volume. If you can't lift

the hair straight up, lift it to the side and dry, using the same technique.

3. Bring the same section of hair down from the top of your head, twirling it around the brush as if it was a strand of spaghetti.

4. Hold the hair down with the brush and move the drier along it.

5. Repeat the same process with the other sections. Never try to dry too large a hunk of hair at once; always work on small sections. (Blow-drying, by the way, is good exercise for the upper arms. If you can't seem to do it right, have it done at a salon and get do-it-yourself instructions from the stylist.)

6. Make sure you leave a little moisture in the hair. It should not be bone-dry. This is essential. You leave the hair damp before you set it for the same reason you would moisten a cotton blouse before ironing. Damp hair will stretch more effectively over the curlers or iron because the hydrogen bonds in it are relaxed. As the hair dries it shrinks, smoothing itself firmly over the curler, creating a tighter curl that holds better. Remember, your hair should be only *slightly* damp and completely dry at the roots closest to the scalp. If you use a curling iron on wet hair, you will burn your scalp.

7. Set your hair on mesh curlers or use a curling iron. Make sure your hair is completely dry before you remove the curlers or stop using the iron. You can only work on a small section of hair at a time with an iron. (*Warning:* Curling irons get very hot and are potentially damaging to the hair.)

Ornamenting the Hair

Indian women adorn their hair with flowers. Etruscan women fastened tiny bells to their braids, which tinkled joyfully as they walked. Egyptian women decorated their plaits with black silk strings and flat ornaments of gold in teardrop shapes, heart shapes, circles, and spools called "bark." Roman women dyed their hair, perfumed it, then powdered it with gold dust. African tribal women, of course, are experts in hair ornamentation, and some wear different colors of beads and strings to signify their social state and state of mind. In one South African tribe, a woman wears red beads in her hair to tell the world she suffers from an intense and jealous passion, or that her eyes are red from weeping for an absent lover. A blue bead says her thoughts fly to the lover wherever he is. Zulu women decorate their top knots with black finch feathers and wear beaded decorations after marriage. Bororo women plait brass coils into their hair, which they have to polish every day.

Try designing personal hair ornaments that express *your* state of mind. Flowers, artificial or real, bells, beads, feathers, gold charms, and cowrie shells can ornament your braids. Tiny safety pins, painted pretty colors, can be hung from cornrows; painted chopsticks can hold chignons in place. Mica powders in glittery shades can be dashed into your hair on special occasions. Gold or silver threads, too, can be woven into braids. Use your imagination to dress up your hairstyle and make it distinctively *you*.

Hot-combing

Hot-combing causes the chemical bonds that create kinky hair to move into a straight line, where they remain until humidity, moisture, or scalp perspiration makes your hair revert to its natural texture. Hot-combing will not damage the hair or scalp if you do it correctly, though pressing too often with too hot a comb can leave your hair thin, limp, and unnaturally shiny. Below is some essential information from expert Ralph Holbrook Micks, my Los Angeles stylist:

1. Make sure your hair is clean and dry before you press; the oil that clings to dirty hair will create an unpleasant odor and may

cause your hair to break when combined with heat. If your hair is wet, you may suffer steam burns.

2. Excess heat *will* damage your hair, so it's vital to heat the comb correctly and test it before using. A small portable electric or gas heater is the proper place to heat your comb because the heat is regulated. The kitchen stove, used by many ladies, doesn't give you enough control over the heating process, and isn't especially sanitary either. Always test the comb on tissue paper before you use it. If the paper scorches or smokes, the comb is too hot. A modern Teflon-coated electric hot comb with a heat setting is a good investment. Remember, the finer your hair the less heat you will need to straighten it. Thick hair needs a hotter comb, but opt for the coolest comb you can use effectively.

3. Press your hair in the direction it grows. A friend can help you do the back if you find it is difficult to reach yourself.

4. It is not necessary to use pressing oil to hot-comb the hair. This tends to make the hair dirty right away because the oil helps collect lint and dust. If you want to use oil, just a minimum of a light-textured cream will do. Too much will "fry" your hair, making it limp and greasy.

5. When you set your hair, use a modern setting gel designed for the black woman; gels will speed up the curling process without making your hair revert like the old-fashioned wet lotions. If you set your hair and dry it under a bonnet drier, use a cool setting; excess heat may make your scalp perspire and your hair revert.

6. Beware of the "Double Press," or a combination of hot comb and curling iron. The superhot curling iron together with the comb gives your hair a lethal dose of damaging heat and may break it.

Relaxing the Hair with Chemicals

Any kind of chemical is risky to use on your hair, especially over a long period of time. Chemically relaxed or permed hair, however, is definitely a convenience for those who prefer straighter styles. A permed style does not require the time-consuming maintenance procedures of heat-relaxed styles and adapts easily to different variations. Chemically treated hair can also be set and cut by any beautician, black or white. Before you perm your hair, however, consider the dangers.

Straighten Means Destroy

The chemical relaxes the hair by destroying the bonds which hold each strand in a kinky configuration. When these bonds are permanently destroyed, the hair can be restructured or straightened. *Destruction,* however, is not a word to take lightly. As the chemical dissolves the kinky bonds, removing and softening them, it also dissolves your *hair,* just as a depilatory dissolves unwanted hair on the body.

The directions on the hair relaxer are the same for everyone. Kinky hair, as we all know, comes in many different textures, and some of us have two or three separate hair textures on our heads, all of which react somewhat differently to the straightener. If you, or your beautician, choose the wrong-strength relaxer for your hair type, or you leave it on too long, you can actually disintegrate your hair or make it so weak it will soon break off close to the scalp. If the relaxer is not used correctly, it also may not work at all, and you will have wasted your time and money.

Touch-ups

Once your hair is chemically straightened it doesn't have to be straightened again—ever! This is why we call it a "permanent." Many people, including professional beauticians, make the mistake of reapplying the chemical to the entire head of hair when regrowth begins. You only have to straighten the regrowth—not the previously straightened hair. Hair that is permed more than once becomes porous and mushy when wet and strawlike when dry; it will break and pop off easily. One of my beautician friends aptly describes such double-permed hair as "garbage." Touch-ups, however, are essential to maintain a permed style because the point at which the straightened hair joins the new, kinky hair is fragile, and when your comb hits it, your hair is liable to break there. Hair is strongest when it remains the same texture for the entire length of the hair shaft.

Leave It to the Pros

Letting a professional perm your hair is no guarantee it will never break. Even beauticians make mistakes when they straighten hair. A professional, however, has the experience and training to know how to control the product and relate it to your particular hair texture and condition.

Doing It Yourself

Because it's a free country we can buy many cosmetic products that are potentially damaging to the hair over the counter—unfortunately! I would love to tell you, "NEVER-NEVER perm your hair yourself," but I know that advice would fall on thousands of deaf ears. Many ladies simply can't afford the expense of having their hair permed in a salon, and are willing to take the risk and do it themselves. Others firmly believe they can do the job as well as anyone. "It's the same product they use in the salon," they rationalize, "and the directions are right on the box." Below are some guidelines for a trouble-free home perm; but no guarantees from Barbara! My tips should also help you decide if your beautician is perming your hair correctly.

1. Only perm virgin hair. Your hair should not be dyed or colored with henna before you relax it. If you've been hot-combing your hair regularly, you must wait two weeks to a month before you perm, depending on the hair's condition. Your hair needs time to recuperate from the heat process. When you hot-comb your hair, the heat from the comb is usually at its most intense a half inch from the scalp, or at the first "bend" of the comb. This part of the hair shaft will be the one most weakened by the heat, and it may break at this point (very close to the scalp)

HERITAGE SECRETS

Relaxing Traditions

There are many ways to relax the hair. Cele women lengthen and straighten the hair by braiding it into stiff plaits. The Swazi people use soap to straighten their hair, rubbing it in and leaving it to form a smooth cap. Other tribes relax their hair with clay or fat, and let water from waterfalls untangle it after washing. In the American South, black people used to straighten their hair by rubbing a string in soot from the fire or laundry and wrapping it tightly around their braids.

when attacked by a chemical. Unless you wouldn't mind having a very short Afro for a while, don't lie to yourself or your beautician. If you've been hot-combing—wait! The reverse is also true; permed hair must grow out before you can use a comb on it. You shouldn't perm your hair if you have any type of sore or abrasion on the scalp either.

2. Select a straightener that contains no lye at all or a low percentage of this product. The chemical name for lye is sodium hydroxide, and it is a powerful but old-fashioned substance that is more damaging to the hair than the new chemical relaxers. Lye is so effective in dissolving hair bonds that it is the main ingredient used in depilatories. Lye can also produce inflammations and eruptions around the hairline and on the scalp. If it gets into the eyes, it damages them *immediately,* possibly permanently. Don't get me wrong: Lye really works, and a product that contains a bit may not be too risky for extremely thick, kinky hair. On the whole, you're safer selecting a product that contains thioglycolate or sulfite-bisulfite instead of sodium hydroxide.

3. Read the directions on the box carefully and apply the product to a test strand of your hair, according to those directions, or to the modified directions in Step 5 below. If the hair on your head has more than one texture, you should really do a test strand on each texture. Separate the strand from your hair with a clip so you won't do it over again when you do the rest of your hair; otherwise you might lose the strand.

4. The directions on relaxers usually tell you to apply the chemical to the back of the hair first. The manufacturers assume

the back is the strongest part of the hair and will therefore resist the relaxer most, enabling it to stay on longer while you apply it to the rest of your head. This may be true for white or Asian people, on whose hair these products are usually tested. Straight hair grows out and drops down in the back, which enables oil from the scalp to roll down the hair shaft, lubricating and strengthening the hair. Our hair, however, grows in an outward direction and is the same strength all over the head. Your hair may be weakest in the back, in fact, because you thwack at this part with a hairbrush, comb it rapidly, sleep on it, or rest your head against the backs of chairs. It is probably safer to apply the relaxer to the side or front of your hair first.

5. I strongly recommend leaving the relaxer on your hair one half to two thirds the amount of time the directions specify. For example, if the directions tell you to leave the product on your hair for ten minutes, leave it on for five to seven minutes. If your hair is extremely thick and kinky, you can leave it on for the whole time—provided you do a test strand first. (Those who plan to leave the perm on less time should also do a test strand so they can gauge how relaxed their hair will be after the process.) If your hair is not relaxed to your satisfaction, wait a couple of days and apply the *same* product to your hair. (Never, never put one type of relaxer on top of another.) Remember, you have already dissolved some of the chemical bonds, and your hair is more porous and better able to receive the second application of relaxer. If you left the relaxer on for five minutes the first time, leave it on for five to seven minutes the second time, certainly not the entire ten minutes, which will overprocess your hair and make it porous, brittle, and liable to break. Today slightly relaxed hair is more fashionable than very, very straight hair for the black woman, so don't overdo it. If you manage to get your hair poker-straight, you may have trouble styling it for months. When it comes to perming, less is better than more.

6. Putting the relaxing solution on the hair is not in itself sufficient to straighten it. The relaxer dissolves the hair bonds, but you must rearrange the strands into a straight line yourself if you want to alter the shape of the hair and remove its curl. You can do this simply with a comb, combing slowly and continuously for ten to twenty minutes. Beauticians can also realign the bonds with water pressure or by manipulating the hair with their hands.

7. Neutralize the hair by rinsing it with water, or by using a neutralizing solution or shampoo contained in the relaxing

product package. Be sure to keep the hair straight and untangled as you neutralize, because this is the process that locks the hair bonds into their new position and you want it to be the right one. If your hair is long, this will be harder to do; enlist the help of a friend.

Know When to Quit

If your do-it-yourself perm is a disaster, don't try it again. Opt for professional service. If the beautician has damaged your hair, go to another one whose clients have healthy, relaxed hair.

Caring for Permed Hair

- Wash permed hair with a shampoo especially formulated for it. Don't use strong dandruff shampoos.
- Condition hair every two weeks with hot-oil treatments. (See "Conditioners" under "Basic Hair Care," page 123.)
- Because relaxed hair is porous you will want to avoid damaging it with hot driers, hot rollers, and curling irons. These are okay for special occasions, but don't make them an essential part of your hairstyling.
- Protect your hair from chlorine, salt water, wind, and sun.
- If the skin at your scalp line is dry or irritated by the relaxer, dab on a solution of Epsom salts in water twice a day until the condition clears up.

The Curly Perm or "Reverse" Perm

The curly perm removes the kinks from the hair and replaces them with curls. A curly perm is a modern, sophisticated look requiring little time-consuming maintenance. This style allows you to wash and set your hair, wash and blow it dry, or wash and let it dry naturally to achieve three slightly different looks.

How It's Done

The curly perm is done with a thioglycolate or "Thil" type of solution. If the hair is kinky, first it is relaxed slightly with the chemical, then it is set on permanent-waving rods and saturated again with the solution so the hair takes the shape of the rod. Then it is dried and neutralized to lock the new curls into place.

Problems, problems

The curly perm sounds simple, but it's not. What it tries to do—straighten and curl the hair at the same time—is not what the product was basically designed to do, which is to curl straight hair. Taking a supertight, kinky curl and restructuring it into a looser, different type of curl is no easy task, even for a modern chemical. Professionals who've been in the beauty business for years hesitate to curly-perm black hair, and those who do have perfected the technique and developed unique methods to compensate for the problems involved. You should never try to create this complicated style at home.

If you were to see a cross-section of a kinky hair, you would find it is shaped like an oval. Straight hair has a round shape. The oval-shaped hair is structurally weaker than the round-shaped hair and is penetrated faster by any chemical and at more points along the hair shaft, creating additional weak points. When this weakened hair is stretched on a rod, even more weak areas are created. In other words, as you loosen your tight curl with the Thil chemical, you make the hair even more fragile than it is normally, and then you put pressure on it by stretching and bending it on a rod. Straight hair, for which the product was designed, can be wound slackly on the curler, which reduces tension on the hair near the scalp. Black hair, however, must be rolled down tightly to the scalp, or the wet solution applied to the rod will cause the hair to kink up tightly, then spring off the curling rod and unwind. When this happens the curl is lost. Weakened hair, stretched, bent, and placed under tension, can break off close to the scalp. Relaxing the hair first, before the perm rods are wound into it, can minimize the danger of breakage but not completely. The curl can also be lost if the Thil solution is left in the hair too long.

Curly-perm Alternatives

Some beauticians achieve a curly-perm look by relaxing the hair slightly, neutralizing it, and simply leaving it with a softened version of its natural curl instead of winding it around rods. The curly look can also be created by finger-shaping damp hair into ringlets with a solution made of half a cup of water mixed with a teaspoon of light oil.

The Fate of the Curly Perm

For mysterious reasons the curly perm tends to have a negative effect on our hair, even if serious breakage does not occur. When straight-haired people get a perm, their hair seems to return eventually to its original texture. Kinky or curly hair, however, never goes back to being kinky or curly once the texture has been chemically damaged. After a while, the ends of the perm dry out and the entire style doesn't look nearly as magnificent as it did at first. As a result, it needs to be trimmed to improve its shape and eliminate the dry ends, then trimmed again. Every time you take your perm to the salon it will get shorter. If you see someone with a long, curly perm, she probably just got it.

Home Care of the Curly Perm

• Two weeks after you have had a curly perm, you should return to the salon to have it checked. If there is damage, point it out to the stylist so she or he can halt it before it gets out of hand. The stylist may want to trim the ends a bit to give the perm bounce and shape.

• A hot-oil treatment should be given after two weeks. You can have this done professionally or do it yourself. (See "Conditioners" under "Basic Hair Care," page 123.)

• The curly perm does not last a year or even six months as many people believe. New growth has to be retouched every two months or so, depending on the growth rate of your hair.

• Wash the curly perm no more than once a week with a mild shampoo.

• If you set your hair, use a lotion that does not contain alcohol, and always protect your hair with end papers.

• When you groom your hair, don't pick it out profusely;

simply lift it lightly with a large-toothed flexible comb. The perm has to be handled with care.

• You may want to use a light pomade or grooming oil in your hair to emphasize its "wet" look. Use just a little; don't overdo it.

• If a professional beautician okays it, a henna or semipermanent rinse can be used on the hair after two weeks.

• Avoid using hot curling irons, hot driers, and hot rollers with this style. Remember, your curly-permed hair is even more fragile than hair that has been simply relaxed.

• You can't have a curly perm if you've recently used a relaxer containing lye on your hair.

STYLING WITH WIGS

A good wig was once a prized possession because it was made from real hair and cost a mint. Cheaper wigs, created from synthetic fibers, were just as popular for a while, though their shiny, artificial-looking strands did not remotely resemble our own hair texture. Today natural looks are in, and the wig is losing its fans; we would rather spend our hair dollars in salons, and are willing to devote more energy to care and styling.

An attractive wig, however, can be fun and save you time at crucial moments when your usual style is a hopeless flop. A wig can also give you a look that is impossible to coax out of your own hair, or it can be worn to give hair damaged from chemical processing a vacation. A wig should never be used to conceal dirty, unkempt hair or to substitute for basic care and conditioning.

Choosing a Wig

1. Choose a wig that matches the texture of your own hair as closely as possible. Even if you've always yearned for straight, shiny hair, a wig in that texture will scream "False!" to everyone.

2. The color of the wig should enhance your complexion. Blond and red hair do not usually go with the black woman's skin tones. Avoid wigs with big, white parts in the center—no one's scalp is that sickly color!

3. The wig should fit correctly. A loose wig will slip and

embarrass you, and a tight wig will choke your hair and scalp. A heavy wig may give you a headache.

4. If possible, have your wig styled to suit your own face and head contours.

Wear and Care of Wigs

1. Because a wig can rub against your scalp and cause you to lose hair in that area, place a little cap made out of a nylon stocking or silk scarf between your hair and the wig. You can also cut a silk band and put it around your head where the wig rests. Pin-curl or braid your own hair before putting on the wig.

2. Wash and style your wig regularly. Experiment with styles, but don't make your wig too extreme or it may broadcast, "I'm a wig," to the world.

3. Use a wig brush to keep your wig well-groomed. I've seen too many ladies wearing wigs that look like mangy old dogs—never attractive, even to a dog lover like me. When your wig has seen better days, bury it and buy another. (Unfortunately, the professional who used to specialize in wig care is part of an almost extinct species. If you can find one, have him or her clean and style your wig professionally.)

4. Try to incorporate some of your own hair at the forehead, where the wig begins—this will make it look more natural. Other hairpieces should always be blended skillfully with your own hair.

5. If you wear a wig to conceal hair damage, take excellent care of your hair. Massage and condition it frequently.

COLORING YOUR HAIR

Coloring your hair can bring out its own natural highlights and the subtle undertones in your skin. Hair can be lightened and the color changed with a permanent dye, which penetrates the protective cuticle, or outer layer, of each hair strand, and then changes the chemical composition that creates the pigment in the inner layer. Temporary or semipermanent dyes and rinses deposit a color on the surface, or cuticle, which eventually washes away.

Permanent Dyes

Beauticians say that lightening or changing the color of dark, kinky-textured hair with a permanent dye is a risky process. Hair dyes are designed for straight-haired people and are tested on them. The color of the dye will penetrate the oval-shaped structure of your kinky hair in a different way than it does straight hair—unevenly. As a result, the color of each hair may not be uniform. When the new hair begins to grow back in its natural color, you will want to retouch it to match the previously dyed hair. This is where real problems begin. It is difficult to apply the dyeing solution to only the new hair. When the previously colored hair comes in contact with the wet dye, it reverts, as kinky hair always does when it meets moisture, and shrinks, pulling the hair you've already colored up into the coloring agent again. It then may happen that you not only lift the color out of your new growth but change the color of the previously dyed hair as well. You may then have hair that has more than one color on each strand. When you go for your second touch-up, the same thing can happen, and you will find yourself with tricolored hair—a cheap, brassy look you never bargained for. (At that point, you will probably opt to have your hair dyed back to its original color.) Since you shouldn't dye hair that has been relaxed, this problem is unavoidable.

Never-Never Number Four

Never try to change the color of your hair with a permanent dye at home. Apart from the problems I've mentioned above, you will have a difficult time selecting a color that will enhance your skin tones. You may be lucky and dye your hair successfully, but the chances are slim. If you must dye your hair, leave it to the pros.

Dying Gray Hair

Gray hair is a sign of old age many of us would like to conceal. A permanent dye can return gray hair to its original color without the same risks involved in lightening or changing hair color. Gray hair, however, is ornery hair to dye because it has a different texture than nongray hair. If a weak dye is used, the gray hair stubbornly resists the color. When a more intense, black dye is used, the hair can absorb it rapidly, and if this dye is left on too long, the fragile gray hair may be destroyed by the chemicals. Don't try it yourself.

Never-Never Number Five

Never try to dye gray hair darker than its original color. Very dark hair has a harsh, aging effect on the face, especially if your complexion is light.

Henna

Henna comes to us from North Africa, where it has been used for centuries to color the hair and create decorative designs on the palms of the hands and feet. Henna is made from a plant, which supplies different shades of dye from its dried and ground stems, leaves, and roots. This natural, semi-permanent dye can be used not only to color your hair, but to condition it, adding body and subtle sheen. Neutral henna (made from the plant's stems) will only condition your hair without adding color. Both black and brown henna will intensify the color of dark hair, and the burgundies and mahoganies will add sophisticated highlights that gleam in the sun. Henna works best on healthy hair and especially well on thin, flyaway hair that needs extra body. It is not recommended for all black hair textures, or for chemically straightened hair that has become porous; henna will make coarse, damaged hair even coarser. If you have doubts, consult your beautician. Sometimes a semipermanent rinse will work better with your hair type than henna. You cannot use henna if you have used other chemicals on your hair, or if you have sores and abrasions on your scalp.

Henna on Gray Hair

Dark hennas will help blend random gray hairs into your head. After the first application, the gray hair will take on some pigment. If the henna treatments are repeated every six weeks, eventually the color will build up on the cuticle until the gray hair is significantly darker than it was. If you use black henna on white hair, however, the hair may turn bluish, an effect you may or may not find attractive. If your hair is more than 15 percent gray, you will not be able to cover it with henna.

Do-It-Yourself Henna With a Friend

It is easiest (and, of course, most expensive) to have your hair hennaed in a salon. The professional will know what shade will bring out the best in your hair and skin, and will also be able to mix different shades for different effects. Some salons mix herbs and fruits and other natural ingredients into the henna for added highlights. I recommend having your hair hennaed once at a good salon; note the type and color of henna used and the procedure, then try it yourself at home.

A friend is necessary to help you apply the henna correctly. She will be able to coat the hair thoroughly with the gloppy henna mixture (one beautician I know calls henna "the messiest thing in beauty"), and apply it evenly in the back. She can also help you rinse it out thoroughly.

What You Need

1. An all-natural brand of henna. Some products labeled "henna" also contain metallic dyes and salts. These can produce a greater variety of colors, but are more apt to make your hair brittle and coarse. Check the package to make sure the henna is pure. If you are trying henna for the first time, avoid the red shades; nothing on the container will tell you how these tones will react with hair in the black color spectrum. Black, brown, neutral, or burgundy are usually safe shades for dark hair. If you have real doubts about the color, try a patch test on a small section of your hair.

2. Rubber gloves.

3. Vaseline petroleum jelly.

4. A small brush with stiff bristles. Color-application brushes are available in beauty-supply stores; you can also use a small hairbrush.

5. Newspaper to place around the floor.

6. A plastic bag or silver foil to place over your head.

7. A good bonnet-type drier.

The Process

1. Wash and thoroughly dry your hair. Use a vinegar rinse (see "After-Shampoo Rinse-Away Conditioners" under "Basic Hair Care," page 123) to shrink and smooth the cuticle of the hair.

2. Boil water and mix it with the henna in a ceramic or glass bowl according to directions on the package. For extra conditioning add an egg. The mixture will be a thick paste like mud. If it gets too stiff as you apply it, add a little more boiling water. If you are using black henna, you can substitute coffee for the water for a more intense effect.

3. Rub Vaseline around your hairline so you won't get "decorative designs" on your skin. Whoever is applying the henna should wear rubber gloves.

4. Have your friend divide your hair into small sections. Beginning close to the scalp, coat each section thoroughly with the henna mixture, using the small, stiff brush. Distributing the henna evenly through the hair is important.

5. When all of your hair is coated with the henna, use the brush to slick it back into a neat "cap" or "helmet."

6. Place the plastic bag over your head or wrap your hair in silver foil. (This is not necessary but will protect your drier hood from henna stains.)

7. Bake the henna on under the bonnet drier for thirty to forty minutes. If you have covered your hair, remove the bag or foil the last twenty minutes. Baking the henna firmly on the hair is the real secret of having it "take." The hair should be hard and completely dry before you rinse the henna off.

8. After you've baked the henna on your hair, wash it off

thoroughly with warm water, rinsing until the water runs clear.

You can repeat the henna process when the color begins to fade, from six weeks to three months.

BASIC HAIR CARE

No style can be beautiful if the hair that creates it is not clean, healthy, and well-groomed. Because our hair is tender, we must nourish and pamper it, carefully selecting shampoos and conditioners that cater to its fragile qualities, and handling it with special care when we style and groom.

Shampooing

Shampoo is designed to strip your hair of dirt and grease. To do this effectively, it must contain a detergent—an alkaline substance we associate negatively with dishpan hands. Detergents, however, are necessary to clean the hair, and come in many strengths and types. All shampoos contain an ingredient called lauryl sulfate; some shampoos are made with one sulfate compound and some have more. In general, the shampoos with fewer sulfates listed in the ingredients are more gentle.

Shampoo for Dry Hair

Most black people have dry hair. Chemical processing tends to make the hair even drier and more porous in texture. Shampoos formulated for dry hair contain fatty substances that reduce the harsh effects of alkaline detergents. If your hair is dry or chemically processed, select a mild shampoo that does not contain alcohol or a large number of sulfate compounds. These shampoos tend to be acidic and shrink the hair cuticle, making it stronger and smoother.

Shampoo for Oily Hair

If your hair is oily, you should wash it with a shampoo designed for oily hair. It should contain more detergents and fewer fatty substances than one formulated for dry hair.

HERITAGE SECRETS

Sweet-scented Hair

In Senegal the pretty ladies combine special grasses, ambergris, and sweet-smelling herbs, then grind them together to make a perfumed incense called *thiouraye,* which they burn in pots in their homes. The *thiouraye* wafts through the house, scenting clothes, bedcovers, and the women themselves, who stand close to the fragrant pots when they want their clothes and hair to gather an especially seductive aroma. To give your own freshly washed hair a sweet, pungent scent, light two sticks of your favorite incense (sandalwood, jasmine, musk, rose, or a combination) and let the perfumed smoke waft into your hair as you dry it with a blow drier, or as you sit with a book, waiting for your hair to dry naturally.

Never-Never Number Six

Never wash your hair with soap of any kind. Some people believe that detergentless shampoos or soaps are gentle; actually, soaps are more alkaline than detergents, harder to rinse off, and leave scummy residues in the hair that make it dry and dull.

Myths and Fairy Tales

Shampoo manufacturers have the best imaginations in the world, and add everything you can name to shampoos to make them different and attractive to the consumer. Beer, eggs, herbs, milk, avocados, apricots, and special proteins and placentas, I'm sorry to say, do little to improve the shampoo's quality, though they often raise its price. Studies have shown these special ingredients don't really improve hair quality because they pass quickly through your hair, then get rinsed down the drain. More important is the balance of detergents, fats, and acids in the shampoo and how they work in relation to your individual hair type. Tests reveal that some shampoos formulated for oily hair actually have more fats and fewer detergents than those formulated for dry hair. No matter what the label says, a shampoo may not work with your hair. If the product you use seems to make your hair oily, dull, or dry, give it to a friend and try another with a *different* list of ingredients. The only way to select a good shampoo for your hair is through trial and error.

How Often to Shampoo

How often you need to shampoo depends on the climate, the place you live, and whether your hair is oily or dry. Dry hair, in general, should be washed no more than once a week and no less than every ten days. Hair tends to absorb odors and the smell of smoke, which is why your freshly shampooed hair may seem soiled again after a night of partying or restaurant dining. Humidity also seems to soil the hair, as does urban pollution. Remember, the people you love smell your hair; it should always be clean and have a pleasant odor. Don't sacrifice cleanliness for the perfection of a hot-combed style.

How to Shampoo

Your kinky, curly hair is delicate and should be handled carefully when you shampoo. Don't rub-a-dub your head as if it were a grease-stained dish towel. Pat the shampoo on and massage it thoroughly but gently into your scalp with your finger-*tips*—no nails or tough little brushes, please. (See "Braiding" in this chapter for information about shampooing this style.) One lather is sufficient unless your hair is very dirty; then you may need two.

Rinsing is an important part of the process. Alkaline substances left in the hair dry it and diminish its glow. Rinse and rinse again, then, just to make sure, rinse a third time. Don't oversoap your hair. A minimum of shampoo is easier to remove.

Conditioners

Regular conditioning helps strengthen the hair and protect it from damage as well as keep it smooth and soft. No conditioner can repair hair that has been eaten away or frayed at the ends by improper care or by chemicals, nor are all conditioners beneficial to every hair type. Below is my list and evaluation of different conditioners.

After-shampoo Rinse-away Conditioners

The Cupboard Miracle: The Vinegar Rinse

The cuticle of kinky-textured hair is made up of tiny, hinged cells, which overlap one another like the scales of a fish. Alkaline shampoos and chemical straighteners make these cells swell and stand out even farther from the hair shaft, giving our hair a rough appearance. An acid substance makes the hair shaft shrink and the "fish scales" lie back down again, smoothing the hair and strengthening it, too. Acid rinses are also cleansers and help rinse away the shampoo residues.

The least expensive and most effective acid rinse comes from your kitchen cupboard. Add four tablespoons of vinegar to a quart of water and shake or stir. Pour the vinegar rinse over your hair after you have showered away all the shampoo. You don't have to rinse the solution off. You can make a similar rinse with lemon juice and water, but lemons are expensive and no more effective than vinegar.

Thyme Herbal Rinse

The herb thyme also has astringent properties and makes a fragrant, cuticle-shrinking rinse for black hair. Boil two tablespoons of whole dried thyme in a quart of water for five minutes and let the "tea" steep. When it is cool, strain it and work the brew into your hair. Rinse with cool water.

The Truth About Balsam Conditioners

Many women use a balsam or cream-type conditioner after they shampoo, which instantly detangles the hair, making it soft and easy to comb. Though these conditioners, which are also acid, seem gentle, the ingredients that attack the tangles also attack the hair, making it lifeless, limp, and dull. They also tend to leave a sticky deposit on the hair shaft that attracts dirt. Cream rinses have an especially negative effect on oily hair. If your hair is dry and gets terribly snarled when you shampoo, the comb you tear through the tangles will do more harm than the cream rinse. Be sure to rinse it off thoroughly, though. You can follow a cream rinse with a vinegar rinse.

Hair-building Conditioners

According to experts, the best conditioners for building and strengthening the black woman's hair are those whose molecules are small enough to penetrate the hair cuticle and sink into the cortex of the hair, where they do their nourishing action until the next shampoo. These conditioners often come in clear liquid form in glass vials which you break. The best ones can usually be identified by their cost—they are expensive! Inexpensive versions of hair-building conditioners may contain drying alcohol or leave a gummy residue on the hair; these aren't much different from setting lotions. Penetrating conditioners are beneficial for thin, flyaway hair or for hair susceptible to damage and breaking.

Hot Oil-conditioning Treatments

Oil conditioners help smooth hair that has been permed or hair that is dry, rough, and porous. A hot-oil treatment every two to three weeks will help keep relaxed hair strong; it will also help strengthen the hair *before* a perm. Commercial oil treatments are easier to remove from the hair, but you can make your own from ingredients in your kitchen.

Sleek Almond Oil Conditioner

1. Shampoo hair once, rinse, and towel dry.
2. Heat a quarter cup of almond oil in a small pan until it's warm, not simmering or boiling. (Hot oil will scald your scalp.) You can also use avocado oil or polyunsaturated vegetable oil; these are fairly easy to remove from the hair.
3. Massage the oil thoroughly into your hair and scalp with the fingertips. You may not need the entire amount.
4. Wrap a warm, wet hand towel around your head and bask under a bonnet-type drier for twenty minutes. If the towel dries out, moisten it with water again.
5. Wash your hair again, applying the shampoo directly to your head without attempting to rinse the oil out with water first.

Sweet Olive Oil Conditioner

This special hair smoother is from my friend Barbara Morris of the B. J. Bubbles Salon in New York, who recommends it for dry or chemically treated hair. The honey has nutritional value, gives the hair sheen, and balances excess acidity, which can cause itching and flaking. The following recipe makes enough for several treatments.

1. Wash hair and rinse.

2. Warm a cup of olive oil with a quarter cup of honey. Pour into a bottle and shake well.

3. Apply two to four tablespoons of the mixture to your hair and scalp, massaging in thoroughly. You may need more if your hair is thick.

4. Cover your head with a plastic cap or bag for one hour, or if you're in a hurry, soak a terry-cloth towel in hot water and wrap your head in it for twenty minutes.

5. Apply shampoo directly to your hair without rinsing it first. You can add an egg to the shampoo, which will help remove the oil from your hair.

(Note—The next time you use the honey-oil mixture, heat it first.)

Protein Conditioners

When your hair is damaged, a protein conditioner fills in and smooths the cracks in the hair shaft. These conditioners also leave dry and chemically treated hair softer and smoother. *Warning:* Overuse can make the hair hard. Good commercial protein conditioners (the package specifies the product is "for dry, brittle or damaged hair") are usually expensive. You can make your own budget versions at home. Some modern hair-setting gels and creams also contain protein conditioners.

Homemade Mayonnaise Protein Conditioner

Mayonnaise, rich in egg protein and oil, makes an excellent conditioner for dry or chemically treated hair. You can use it from the jar, or make a more pleasant, additive-free version in your blender.

How to Prepare

1. Break an egg into the jar of a blender. Blend thirty seconds until foamy.

2. Add one tablespoon of vinegar and blend ten seconds more.

3. Uncover the jar and, still blending at a slow speed, pour one cup of olive, avocado, sesame, almond, or polyunsaturated vegetable oil into the egg-and-vinegar mixture slowly so it won't splatter. (You can also combine two different kinds of oil.) If you like add a couple of drops of your favorite scented oil or perfume. When the mayo is thick, it is ready to use.

How to Use

1. Massage the mayonnaise into your dry, clean hair and cover with a plastic bag. The heat from your own head will be contained by the plastic and help the mayonnaise penetrate your hair.

2. Leave the mayonnaise on for at least a half an hour. I do my housework with the mayonnaise-bag combination on my head (and hope no one important rings my doorbell).

3. Apply a mild shampoo directly to your head without rinsing first, then wash and rinse thoroughly.

Potent Guacamole Conditioner (for Oily Hair)

This conditioner will remove extra oil from your hair and leave it lustrous and easy to style. Combine a tablespoon of brewers' yeast with half a medium-sized avocado. Add an egg yolk and two teaspoons of neutral henna and mash thoroughly or blend in your blender. Massage into your hair and scalp. Leave the mixture on for an hour, then shampoo out.

Rosemary Highlight Conditioner

Rosemary makes an excellent conditioner for dark hair, bringing out pretty highlights and adding shine. The special oil in the herb is also beneficial to the hair. In fact, some health-food stores and cosmetic specialty shops sell the pure form of the oil and shampoos and rinses made from it. To make your own rosemary rinse, boil two tablespoons of dried rosemary in one quart of water and steep until the mixture is dark in color. When cool, strain and work into your clean hair. Rinse lightly. The scent that will linger on is interesting.

HERITAGE SECRETS

African Butter Conditioner

All over Africa, women condition their skin and hair with a special cosmetic butter. In Ghana the butter is called *shea,* and in Senegal, *karite.* It is made from various sources, including nuts and seeds. In Ethiopia the special butter is made from milk. If you want to try the African butter treatment, take some plain softened butter and massage it into your head the night before you shampoo. Place a plastic bag over your head to protect your bedclothes. The next morning shampoo and rinse. The butter should make your hair soft and glowing. You can also try butter on your skin.

Myths and Fairy Tales

Do you still rub grease or oil into your hair? If so, I'd advise you to give up this antiquated custom. Black people first began oiling their scalps because they believed this practice made their hair less dry, and straighter and shinier. First of all, black hair isn't supposed to shine the way straight hair does. Small bubbles in the hair shafts enable kinky hair to diffuse and refract light—for a subtle matte glow that is part of our special beauty. Extra grease on the scalp does not make the hair less dry, but actually blocks the sebaceous glands, preventing the natural oils from flowing and lubricating the hair and scalp; the result is drier, not oilier hair. Though the extra oil may prevent your hair from losing moisture, it also keeps moisture from the environment out. Worse, grease and oil make the hair smell unpleasant and attract dust and dirt, transforming the head into a mop. Finally, grease can work its way into the hair follicles, causing a bacterial infection called *folliculitis,* which could result in bald patches. Convinced? Go modern and stop oiling your hair.

Castor Oil Rub

If you have a curly perm, or feel your hair needs just a touch of extra oil to maintain its style or special look, use only a very small amount of a light, lubricating oil. Castor oil is ideal for this purpose, and many black people firmly believe it makes the hair grow.

To oil the hair properly, part it and apply a *tiny* amount to the scalp, spreading it with your index finger. Then brush your hair to distribute the oil thoroughly along the hair shaft. You should never add so much oil to your hair that it lacks the spring and movement essential to today's styles.

Massaging the Scalp

People with dry hair and scalps can help their natural oils flow with regular scalp massage. Though massage does not make the sebaceous glands produce more oil, it does unclog the pores, freeing the existing oil and distributing it along the hair shaft. Massaging also improves circulation in the scalp, bringing more nutrients and moisture to the hair follicles, and rids the pores of deposits that may cause dandruff. An electric scalp massager is a great gift to ask for or give. You can also massage your hair with your fingers once a week before shampooing. Here's how:

1. Lift your hair and put your fingertips on your scalp.
2. Use your fingertips, fingers, and palms to knead the scalp all over your head, lifting it and moving the skin as much as possible.
3. Placing your palms on your scalp, knead it by contracting your hands.
4. Rotate the fingers and thumbs in small circles all over your scalp, using pressure. Don't forget to massage the hairline at the front and back of your head.

Simple Upside-down Massage

One of the easiest ways to bring blood to your scalp is to lie on your bed and let your head, upper chest, and arms dangle off the edge of the bed toward the floor. Relax and remain in this position for five minutes.

Brushing the Hair

The oil secreted by our scalps has a hard time flowing down our hair unless we help it with a brush. Brushing distributes oil along the hair shaft, helping to strengthen and condition the ends. Brushing also grooms the hair and removes dust and dirt between washings.

Selecting a Brush

A brush with firm, round, wide-spaced boar's bristles is your best selection. The bristles should not be too hard or stiff. If your hair or scalp is tender, choose a brush with soft bristles. Less expensive brushes with sharp nylon bristles will tear at your hair and absorb less of the dirt and dust than natural bristles, which have an uneven surface. Before you buy a brush, test it on the inside of your arm. If it pricks your skin unpleasantly, it will also prick your scalp.

How Often to Brush

Brushing once to three times a week, twenty-five strokes at a time, is sufficient. The proverbial one hundred strokes a day will do your delicate hair more harm than good.

How to Brush

Use long, slow, relaxed strokes. Sit on a bed or chair, put your head between your knees, and brush the underside of your hair. Then brush the top of the hair, parting and sectioning it first. Make sure to include the hair closest to the scalp in your stroking; this is where the oil secreted by the scalp is located, and you want to move it down the hair shaft.

Combing

Excess combing and picking can cause kinky hairs, wrapped around each other, to break. Always use a flexible, plastic comb with wide-spaced teeth that won't catch in the tangles and break them off. Avoid constant, compulsive combing, especially if you wear your hair in a natural style or if it is damaged.

Black hair, left in its natural texture, tends to become tangled when wet. Always extract the tangles as gently as possible; don't hack at them with impatient swipes of the comb. You can also brush your hair when it's wet. Separate the tangled section by parting your hair and slowly ease the comb through the snarls. Massaging shampoo in thoroughly when you wash can eliminate tangling.

The Hair Diet

Hair, like any other part of your body, is nourished by the food you eat. Once hair grows out of the scalp it is dead and does not respond to internal conditions; but new hair, incubating in the follicles beneath the scalp, benefits from a good diet. Eating the following foods should improve the quality of your hair, especially if they've been absent from your diet.

HERITAGE SECRETS

Food for the Hair

Japanese and Korean women, famed for their strong hair, have always believed that seaweed and sesame oil strengthen the hair from the inside out. Add a tablespoon of unrefined sesame oil to your salads (a delicious, nutty taste) and try some of the flat, black seaweed called *nori* or *laver* (available in health-food stores and Oriental food shops) wrapped around a slice of cheese for a tasty hors d'oeuvre.

---

1. Protein

Your hair, like your nails, is basically composed of a protein, and needs plenty of that substance to live and grow. Good protein sources are meat, fish, poultry, eggs, milk, soybeans (including *miso* and bean curd), and brewers' yeast. One of the best hair foods, loaded with both protein and Vitamin B, is liver. If you are a vegetarian, you may not be getting the protein you need. Try adding bean curd combined with sesame seeds or peanut butter with whole wheat bread to your diet for an excellent source of nonanimal protein.

2. Fatty Acids

An important smoother for the hair (and skin) is the fat obtained from vegetable oils. These vegetable fats, which are good for you, should not be confused with high-calorie butter fat or meat fat, which are not. Crash diets that ask you to eliminate all fats from your diet for any period of time (longer than a week) are potentially damaging to your hair. Without a regular supply of fatty acids, the hair can grow rough and fragile. A tablespoon of unrefined vegetable oil (soybean oil, sesame oil, avocado oil, corn oil, etc.) every day may add strength and luster to dry, flyaway hair.

3. Vitamin A

When your body is short of Vitamin A, your hair will become weak and lose its natural glow. Dandruff can also be a result of a Vitamin A deficiency. Fish liver oils are the richest commercial source of Vitamin A. Adding a good supply of carrots, deep-green leafy vegetables (like watercress and spinach—not pale, anemic iceberg lettuce) to your diet should improve your hair. Parsley is a good source of Vitamin A, too, and helps cleanse the kidneys and bladder of impurities. Always take your Vitamin A naturally unless a doctor tells you that you have a deficiency. Too many vitamin supplements can be toxic.

Troubleshooting

Below is a list of problems that plague black hair, along with the causes and some cures. I've mentioned some of the information before in different contexts, and some of it is new; I don't think I can stress too strongly the importance of strong, healthy hair and the ways to make it yours.

Problem: Dry, Brittle, Flyaway Hair That Breaks Off Easily and Splits at the Ends

Possible Cause: Using Too Much Heat on the Hair

Excessive or incorrect use of blow driers, curling irons, hot combs, and hot rollers. Nervous tension can also damage the hair.

Solution

Use the lowest setting on your electrical appliances to avoid heat damage. If you use hot rollers, the least damaging are recent models, which have a misting device built in. These misters put some of the moisture back into the hair that the heat takes away as it curls. If you have an older, nonmisting unit, try moistening an end paper in water before you roll the curler into your hair. (See "Relaxing With Heat" in this chapter for additional information.)

Possible Cause: Exposure to the Elements

Wind, sun, heat, salt water, and chlorine can frazzle the hair. Permed hair is especially susceptible to the elements.

Solution

Cover your hair with a loose-fitting hat when exposed to the heat, cold, or wind. Wear a scarf or hat in the sun. Always wear a bathing cap when you swim in salty or chlorinated water. Applying a penetrating conditioning cream to your hair before you swim will also protect it. Wash all the water out of your hair carefully. Saunas and steam rooms will also dry your hair; use a conditioner and wear a shower cap when you indulge.

Possible Cause: Setting Incorrectly

Sponge rollers are damaging to kinky-textured hair because they suck up moisture, crinkling the hair like a piece of silver foil. Sleeping on curlers is extremely damaging to your hair as well as to your head and dreams. Bobby pins and permanent-waving rods also damage the hair when used too frequently.

Solution

Use magnetic or wire-mesh rollers. A setting gel, designed for black hair, will help the curl take hold faster and eliminate the time your hair must be stretched on rollers. Avoid making permanent-waving rods an everyday essential for a fluffy Afro style.

Possible Cause: Harsh Shampoos, Conditioners, and Setting Lotions

When you switch to a new shampoo, conditioner, or setting lotion, check the list of ingredients and keep a close watch on your hair. If your hair becomes noticeably drier, discontinue the new product and select another with a different list of ingredients. Avoid any product that contains alcohol or a large number of sulfate compounds.

HERITAGE SECRETS

Caribbean Coconut Sun Conditioner

In the Caribbean, ladies know that the intense ultraviolet rays of the summer sun can scorch the hair as well as the skin. They take a common product, the oil of a coconut, and rub it into their hair before venturing outdoors. The warmth of the sun in combination with the moisturizing properties of the oil adds luster and softness to their hair. Coconut oil is available in health-food stores. Try it as a conditioning sunscreen for your hair.

Problem: Porous Hair That Breaks Easily

Possible Cause: Overprocessing With Chemicals

By now you should be aware that any kind of chemical is potentially damaging to the hair. Below are some of the reasons why the chemical may have damaged your hair.

• You had your hair permed after you had been hot-combing it regularly.

• You colored and permed your hair at the same time. Even a semipermanent rinse or henna treatment can affect permed hair badly.

• You used one kind of relaxer on top of another.

• You failed to retouch the regrowth, which placed stress on your hair shaft and caused your hair to break.

• Instead of perming the regrowth only, you permed your entire head again. Once hair is permed, it doesn't have to be permed again.

• You are allergic to chemicals, and they make your hair break off.

• You used hot driers, curlers, and curling irons on your permed hair.

• You didn't condition your hair regularly with oil treatments or penetrating protein conditioners.

• You combed and brushed too frequently.

Solutions

If your hair is damaged, give the chemicals a rest. Try consulting a top stylist to discover what your natural texture can do for you instead of fighting it constantly. You may have to cut your hair very short at first to get rid of the damage, but eventually it will grow in longer and stronger. Then if you still want straighter hair, put yourself in the hands of a first-rate professional who has a good reputation for producing healthy permed hair.

Problem: Hair That Is Limp, Lifeless, and Drab

Possible Cause: Using Too Hot a Hot Comb and Too Much Pressing Oil for Your Type of Hair (Especially If It Is Thin and Fine)

Solution

Try a Teflon-covered hot comb with a heat setting, or make sure your regular iron is cooler. Test it first. Try pressing without using oil.

Possible Cause: Using a Cream-type Conditioner

Solution

Switch to a vinegar rinse and comb the tangles out of your hair carefully.

Possible Cause: Oiling Your Hair the Old-fashioned Way

Solution

Instead of oiling, massage your scalp and brush your hair to distribute the natural oils. If you must use oil, apply a minimum of a light variety.

Problem: Hair That Was Once Dry or Normal and Is Now Too Oily

Possible Cause

If you've recently permed your hair, the oil from your scalp may now be flowing freely down your straightened hair shaft, uninhibited by the crooked freeways of kinks and curls. You now see the oil you didn't notice before.

Solution

Change to a shampoo designed for oily hair. Brushing with a brush wrapped in cheesecloth will also help remove extra oil from the hair between shampoos.

Possible Cause: Overuse of Deep-penetrating or Oily Conditioners

Solution

Too much of a good thing can be just as bad as not enough. Even if your hair is dry you don't need a deep-conditioning treatment more than every two or three weeks. If your hair suddenly seems oily, you may be overdoing it, or you may not be getting the oily conditioner out.

Possible Cause: Change of Weather or Hormonal Balance

Everyone's hair (like everyone's skin) can change its character with age and with changes in internal balances. Hair often seems to become drier in the dry cold, or in response to indoor heating, and oilier in hot, humid weather.

Solution

Change the type of shampoo and conditioner you use.

Problem: Dandruff

Possible Cause

A little dandruff is normal because extra skin cells on the scalp naturally flake away and fall off. Both dry and oily scalps develop dandruff. Microorganisms can cause the abnormal clumping together of excess scalp cells, and some dandruff is actually a skin disease called seborrheic dermatitis, or psoriasis. Stress, too, can aggravate dandruff, as well as scratching your scalp with your fingernails.

Solution

Brush your hair before shampooing; this should help loosen the flakes and make it easier to wash them away. If your dandruff becomes an embarrassing snowfall, use a special dandruff shampoo containing zinc pyrothione. *(Warning:* Dandruff shampoos can be drying.) If the condition fails to improve, see a dermatologist. A regular vinegar rinse and scalp massage should help those with oily-scalp-type dandruff. You can also try an antidandruff herbal rinse made by boiling two tablespoons of dried nettle in a quart of water for a few minutes. Cool, strain, and work into the scalp.

Possible Cause: Hair Sprays and Setting Lotions

Some dandruff is actually artificial flakes created by the overuse of hair sprays or setting lotions, which can contain sugar. These sticky, sweet sprays can also attract parasites if they remain in the hair too long.

Solution

If you use hair sprays and setting lotions regularly, once a month boil a quarter cup of baking soda in a quart and a half of water and let the mixture cool. When it is tepid, work it through your hair after shampooing, then rinse it off thoroughly with clear water. The baking soda solution will strip excess residues from your hair.

Problem: Graying Hair

Possible Cause: Heredity

When your hair begins to gray and how fast it grays is largely determined by a genetic program. In other words, you will probably find gray hairs in your head about the time one of your parents did.

Solution

There's no way to stop Mother Nature from doing her work. Gray streaks in your hair can be very attractive, an interesting sign of maturity. If you don't like it, see a good colorist. As I mentioned before, gray hair is tricky to dye and needs professional attention.

Possible Cause

Occasionally, prematurely gray hair is due to a lack of B vitamins in the diet, particularly the one known as PABA.

Solution

If you suspect your hair is graying too fast, adding a PABA supplement to your diet (it must be prescribed by a doctor) or taking two tablespoons of brewers' yeast in juice three times a day may slow the graying process down. (Brewers' yeast is a rich source of B vitamins and contains traces of PABA. Even if it doesn't stop you from graying, it certainly won't hurt you.)

Problem: Hair Loss or Balding

Possible Causes

Everybody loses a certain number of hairs every day because once hair grows, it goes into a resting phase and eventually falls, soon to be replaced by a new strand of hair. Hair left in its natural texture loses from forty to sixty strands a day, but chemically treated hair loses from fifty to seventy-five strands. Almost every woman's hair thins with age. A very few women become bald because of hereditary patterns, like men do. Hormone or endocrine disorders, diseases of the scalp, and infections in the hair follicles will cause balding, too. Temporary hair loss may follow childbirth, high fevers, surgery, radiation, and chemotherapy, as well as other medical treatments.

Solutions

If you find your hair growing abnormally thin or developing bald patches, consult a dermatologist immediately. Your condition may well be curable, but embarrassment or hesitation to discuss it with a doctor may allow it to progress. Hair transplant operations can now replace hair in bald areas of the scalp. Remember, if your hair is very thin, the shorter you cut it the more you will seem to have.

Possible Cause

Hair breakage is often mistaken for hair loss. Tight braids and chignons or allergies to chemicals may cause you to lose hair. Some women lose it along the hairline at the temple because that is the first place the comb hits and with the greatest force. A lot of breakage will make the hair look thinner. Temporary hair loss can become permanent if the cause is not eliminated.

Solution

If your hair is breaking, handle it with care. Pat it dry after shampooing. Groom with a comb and brush only when absolutely necessary. Opt for a natural style that gives your hair relief from heat, chemicals, and rollers. Braids and chignons should not pull at the scalp or hairline.

4

Dressin' Up

WE HAVE STYLE

We black women have an intuitive understanding of clothes and how to wear them. We've always known how to take plain old green money (a lot or a little) and transform it into a gorgeous outfit that catches all eyes. We know how to choose colors, how to combine lines, textures, and accessories, and how to add the extra-special touch that wins admiration everywhere. We aren't afraid to say, "Clothes make the woman," because we know the way we dress tells the world something important about who we are.

MY LOVE AFFAIR WITH CLOTHES

I happen to love clothes, and clothes are important to me. A Rolls-Royce just doesn't impress me, but a beautiful, well-put-together, stylish outfit does. I like to change my wardrobe frequently, and if the latest style does something for me, there's no way it won't find its way to my closet soon. As a child I discovered that when my mother dressed me up in a frilly party dress, my younger brother, usually busy practicing wrestling holds on me, backed off and showed a new respect. Since then, pretty, feminine clothes have always made me feel special and important, like a queen bee.

When I was an actress I began to think of clothes as costumes that helped me communicate the essence of certain roles. Today my busy career still has me playing many roles. The clothes I wear help me relate to different people and different situations effectively. For example, when I appear in a department store to promote my line, I choose a practical but elegant costume that relays the glamorous feeling of my cosmetic products to my customers. When I visit a school to talk to kids about grooming, I want them to be able to touch me, shake my hand, and put their arms around me; an overly sophisticated look would put them off, so I opt for a simple skirt, blouse, and blazer combination. When I'm invited to a dinner for an important someone, I might appear in a chic, all-black gown, and wrapped in a dramatic stole or cape. My TV and radio appearances require yet another version of myself, and another costume. Because an average day might involve more than one of these activities, I've learned to change the mood of a basic outfit with shoes, hats, and other accessories. Before I leave my house, I always look in the mirror and ask myself if the Barbara Walden I see reflected there is the appropriate Barbara for my day.

Every woman, I believe, has more than one important role to play, and her clothes should help her act the parts. Whether she is a wife, mother, teacher, or businesswoman by day, she is bound to be someone different at night. Her clothes should be as versatile as she is, and communicate the spirit of her profession and unique inner life.

THE CLOTHES HUNT

Though I love clothes, I hate to shop for them. My wardrobe is so crucial to my work that selecting new garments can become a tension-producing event. To buy the clothes I want and need with the fewest headaches, then, I've had to devise a special shopping system. I've discovered that some serious preliminary thought and a mental checklist of important facts to consider prevent me from buying "mistake" garments I never really wear.

OPEN EYES SHOPPING TIPS

1. Keep an Eye on Style

There is scarcely a woman alive who doesn't want to have some kind of style because contemporary clothes communicate a contemporary person. I look forward to changes in fashion because I can use them to emphasize the changes in myself. Below are three ways to keep yourself abreast of current fashions.

• *Study style in fashion magazines*

"Style" is not just a different skirt length or a new silhouette in jackets or pants; it is the special way the new lines and lengths are combined. The layouts in fashion magazines are designed by stylists who are experts at putting garments and accessories together into a unified look. When you read your favorite magazine, notice how the separates are selected to look well together. Notice what type of shoes the stylist has chosen to enhance the look of skirts, dresses, and pants. Notice the width of belts, the shapes of purses, and the textures and styles of jewelry. You don't have to copy the look you see in a fashion magazine exactly, but it should help you decide what a fashionable look is and how to create one.

• *Study style in your favorite stores*

The buyers in chic shops have an innate sense of what will be "in" the following season; they see all the latest fashions and select them for the racks before that season really begins. A regular tour of departments in large stores and boutiques that seem to cater to your taste should keep you abreast of incoming styles.

• *Study style on the street*

Some of the most contemporary and interesting styles never appear in fashion magazines, but are worn by especially innovative individuals I call "stylemakers." You will find the stylemakers at parties, restaurants, and parks. You may have a friend with a special fashion savvy, too. If you see or know someone with unique and exquisite taste, take time out to analyze the way she puts herself together. With a little study and imagination, you can become a stylemaker yourself.

Your study of style should give you a good idea what new garments you will need to update your present wardrobe. Ask yourself which of the new fashions you identify with your personality and taste. If you can afford to buy everything you want, painful decisions will not be necessary. If there's a limit to your clothing budget, however, decide what new style of garment will work with the clothes you already have to give you the contemporary look. Shopping is easier when you have a definite idea of what you are looking for. Remember, you can and *should* change your mind if the new style doesn't look right on you.

2. Keep an Eye on Color

The first thing that catches my eye in a garment is its color. Possibly because I've studied painting, I know how to create surprising but effective color combinations. Color excites me, and I know how to use different colors to create different feelings.

The first thing any black woman should ask herself when she's buying a garment is, "What does the color do for my skin?" The color of your clothes, like the cosmetics you wear, should enhance the undertones of your complexion and make its unique beauty come alive. Don't buy a color just because you like it but because when you see yourself wearing it, you know it really does something for you. In my opinion, clear, bright colors electrify dark skin. Most black women, I believe, should avoid deep navy blues, very dark browns, or dark, dreary grays; these colors make our complexions look dull. Below are some approaches to consider for your wardrobe.

• *Choose a color and make it your trademark*
Yellow has always been a happy color for me, and I wear a lot of it. (Once actor Johnny Forsythe saw me wearing my bright-yellow angora sweater in a gift shop and commented, "Barbara, you look just like a delicious yellow ice cream cone." I loved looking "delicious"!) You may want to make one color the theme of your wardrobe. Different colors connote different moods to different people. To me, red and yellow are brave, joyful colors; purples and wines are regal; black is sophisticated; and blues and greens are serene, like the sea. Find a color and identify with it.

Remember, there are many tones of each color which can be worn together. An all-blue, red, or white outfit can be daring and glamorous.

• *Base your wardrobe on three mixable colors*
If your clothing budget is low, you can stretch it by buying all

your garments in three shades that mix and match. Beige, wine, and blue is a good "mixable" combination. If you can wear the same pants or skirt with two different shirts and blazers, you will get the maximum number of looks from a small wardrobe. You can accessorize with bright scarves, shoes, and belts to stretch your look even farther. Even if you have scads of clothes, packing mixables which all go together is a good way to save suitcase space when you travel.

• *Specialize in outrageous combinations*

Orange and mauve, vivid aqua and black, yellow and red are all combinations that can look gorgeous together—believe it or not! If you are an outgoing, innovative lady, express your vivacious personality in your approach to color. Don't settle for timid-but-true color combinations. I had a stunning dress made in blue and green long before any designer officially approved of the combination, and it opened eyes everywhere. The color combination that seems to defy all logical rules is often the most interesting. As long as colors don't clash (or give you a distinctly queasy feeling in the pit of your stomach) they go together. If you are the type of lady who can carry off a witty combination, try the yellow and black of the bumblebee, the jewel-like blues, greens, and wines of the peacock, or wear tiger- and leopard-print pants and skirts with vivid blouses. (One tip: the finer and more subtle the fabric, the better any wild color will look.)

3. Keep an Eye on Fabric

Your approach to fabric should reflect your overall approach to clothes. If you hate to shop, prefer classic styles that have staying power, and seldom throw anything away, you will want to invest in better fabrics. I've always felt that in the long run expensive fabrics are bargains because they last forever, launder and clean well, and hold their shape. Pure silks, cottons, linens, and wools get a lovingly worn look with age. On the other hand, if your clothing budget is low, and you like to change your wardrobe frequently and stay in the height of style, less expensive or synthetic materials may be for you. Some of the new synthetics, like imitation leather and shiny, "wet look" blends, have a sure-fire "Now" look. Remember, inexpensive wool blends and

polyesters will tend to form "pills," or little balls of fabric, with
laundering and wear. Fabrics that are stiff like cardboard and
don't flow with the body, or are definitely sleazy, will never look
elegant.

My own wardrobe is made of almost 100 percent pure, natural materials. I love fabrics made out of "all" something—including real furs. I enjoy touching these rich, luxurious fabrics and feeling them caress my body. Yet I know women who can buy and sell me twice who won't wear anything but polyesters. One friend of mine, a well-known fashion designer, wouldn't think of buying a garment she couldn't wash out in the sink of her hotel. Many of the new polyesters and rayons, synthetic matte jerseys, and wool blends are fine-looking and cost almost as much as natural fabrics. They are, however, easier and cheaper to care for. Always check the label and know what fabric you are bringing home and the type of care it requires. If a particular material doesn't wear well, don't buy it again.

Before you buy a garment, ask yourself the following questions about the fabric:

• *Will it shrink?*

If the garment is Sanforized, it will not shrink more than 1 percent when washed and line-dried. The term "preshrunk" also assures you of minimal shrinkage. The labels on some fabrics advise you not to dry them in an electric drier; this indicates a good possibility of shrinkage. If you're buying an expensive all-cotton or polyester-cotton blend which does not specify "preshrunk" or "Sanforized" on the label, get it a size larger than you need.

• *Will it wrinkle?*

Crush the fabric in your hand. If it wrinkles or already looks wrinkled in the store, it is not crease-resistant and will not look crisp and neat when you wear it. Keep in mind that some fine fabrics, like handkerchief linen and cotton-linen blends, are not meant to look crisp.

• *Will it fade?*

Check the label to see if there is any information about the colorfastness of the garment. The term "vat dyed" is a sign of quality color. If the garment is a pure, natural fabric like cotton or linen that you should be able to wash, and the label specifies "dry clean only," the color may fade when it touches water. Dark colors often fade on inexpensive, imported fabrics, too. (See "Tender Loving Clothes Care" on page 154 for a color-fast test.)

• *Will it pill?*

If the polyester-blend or wool-blend garment is already sprouting tiny balls of material on its surface, it will pill even more with wear and care. Some fine wools, like cashmere, also pill. You can rub the fabric against itself to see if the pills form. (Regular brushing of wool garments with a clothes brush will minimize pilling.)

• *Are there flaws?*

Some fabrics have lines of thread or pulls and discolorations. If the garment is marked "irregular" or is available at a discount price, check it carefully for fabric flaws.

• *Does it itch or scratch?*

Some people are allergic to some fabrics or find them uncomfortable. If the garment pesters your skin, you will never wear it. Don't buy.

4. Keep an Eye on Fit and Cut

The true elegance of a garment lies in the majesty of its lines and the way it fits. In general, expensive garments fit the best, though a pricey dress or skirt may simply not be made for your particular figure. A garment that is cut well and really fits will make you look slender and svelte and will hang gracefully on your body without bulging or buckling in the wrong places. You will find that different designers' clothes fit your individual proportions differently; try on garments made by a wide variety of manufacturers until you find one who seems to make his fashions just for you.

Below is a "Good Fit Checklist" to keep in mind when you're shopping:

• Different styles of pants should be worn at different lengths. Pants should not be too short for the style and should not fit too tightly. If they "cup" your behind, emphasize bulges on the sides of the hips or abdomen, or grab at the crotch, they are too tight for you. Try sitting, walking, and squatting in pants before you buy. If one size is too tight and the next size is too loose, it is better to buy the loose pair and have them altered than to buy the pair that begs you to lose five pounds. (Nobody sees the disposable label that says Size 14, but they do see the pants on your body.)

• Jackets, blouses, and sweaters should fit comfortably in the armhole, and the line of the garment's shoulder should correspond with your own shoulder line. Long sleeves should reach just below the bones in your wrist. Shirts shouldn't gap when buttoned, nor should their tails be too short to tuck into skirts and pants. A jacket should not be cut longer or shorter than its style dictates.

• Thank heavens, fashion designers have given up telling us our hemlines are all wrong for this (or any other) season, and we are now free to wear our skirts at the length we like best. When you buy a dress or skirt, however, it should not be too short for its line. That is, if the skirt is meant to be worn just below the knee and is cut to look most fashionable and graceful at that length, don't buy it if the hem hits your knee at the middle of the kneecap. You can take a new skirt up, but it's harder to let it down without leaving a sloppy, telltale line. A skirt will be uncomfortable if it pinches at the waist. If it's styled slim, you should be able to walk in it without feeling hobbled.

• Dresses should fit comfortably in the armhole and not ride up at the waist when you lift your arms.

• Coats should fit loosely enough to be worn over sweaters. The armhole should be roomy, and there should be plenty of give across the chest and back. A tight coat will always look skimpy and cheap, no matter how much you paid for it.

A Footnote About Shoes

We love high heels because they make our bodies and legs look slender and sexy. But however gorgeous those stiletto heels look in the mirror, they won't look pretty if they send you staggering ungracefully down the street. No shoe that is uncomfortable to wear is worth the leather it's made of. An uncomfortable shoe can cause backaches, ingrown toenails, disfiguring corns and bunions on the feet, and it can twist your once lovely face into a mask of pain. To make sure shoes fit when you buy them. . .

• Always walk in shoes you plan to buy on an uncarpeted area of the store. You may have to travel to find one because most shoe stores carpet themselves to the hilt, knowing full well shoes feel better on soft surfaces.

• A shoe should not bulge when you stand in it, or leave noticeable gaps between your foot and the leather along the sides or at the heel. The back of your foot should not move up out of the heel when you walk. There should also be a space (about a half inch) between the tip of your large toe and the tip of the shoe.

Never-Never Number One

Never buy a shoe that hurts in the store, thinking you will break it in at home. Believe me, it will break *you* long before you break it.

• Shoes with high heels should be balanced correctly. This means the shoe sits evenly on the floor when your foot isn't in it and doesn't teeter when you wear it.

• Invest your shoe dollars in quality, not quantity. Good shoes are a bargain no matter how much they cost. A comfortable dress shoe in a basic color of fine, soft leather and in a sandal or pump style will never go totally out of fashion. A good pair of boots, too, will last for years, provided you give soles, heels and leather the proper attention. (See "Tender Loving Clothes Care.")

5. Keep an Eye on the Construction

A well-made garment will hold its shape and won't develop sags in the hem or seat, raveling threads, and split seams. Before you buy anything, turn it inside out and check . . .

• *The zipper.* If the garment has a zipper, the fabric around it should not be puckered, and the zipper should lie flat and open and close easily. The zipper should allow you enough room to get in and out of the garment without straining the seams.

• *The seams and darts.* Seams should not be split on the garment before you buy it. If they are, it's a sign that the thread used to sew them was weak, or the stitches are too large or too small. The seams should be at least a half inch wide and should be finished so their edges do not ravel. Prints, stripes, and plaids should be matched at the seams. Darts should end in a fine point and fall where they are supposed to fall on your body. (This is a sign of good fit as well as good construction.)

• *The lining.* Quality garments, especially those made out of fabrics which stretch or wrinkle, should be lined. Nowadays, however, even major designers of very expensive clothes often fail to line their garments. (A garment may be left unlined to allow its fabric to fall fluidly.) Any close-fitting skirt, dress, or pants will develop a bulging seat unless it is lined. Make sure to check the lining of the coat you buy; a warm lining means a warm coat.

6. Keep an Eye on Your Budget

Smart shopping can get you more clothes instead of less for the same money. Do take advantage of sales. Department stores must reduce the previous season's stock in order to clear the racks for the next season's garments. Summer clothes go on sale on Memorial Day, winter clothes around Thanksgiving, and holiday merchandise the day after Christmas. Columbus Day is traditional "Coat Sale Day." The first reductions are from 25 to 40 percent, but if you wait yet another month you can pay as little as a half or a third of the original asking price. Boutique sales begin a month later than department store sales. Fine designer garments can be had on sale for the same price as more ordinary clothes at the beginning of the season. Other ways to get the most for your shopping dollars . . .

• Seek out discount stores that sell designer clothes at a lower cost than regular stores and boutiques. These places, often advertising "high fashion at reduced prices," do not offer you the convenience of elegant stores, but they give you fine garments for less money.

• Don't dismiss thrift shops and flea markets. They are a good source of discounted merchandise and elegant castoffs that may be perfect in your own wardrobe. A friend of mind, who bought a beautiful fox jacket for thirty-five dollars at the Salvation Army, calls it her "Sally Ann" creation.

• If you can't afford clothes in the finest fabrics and designs, try them on in the designer department of your store, then look for "knockoffs," or less expensive imitations of the same styles, in the budget section of the store. Seventh Avenue manufacturers copy famous designers' hit styles in cheaper fabrics. The tailoring will not be quite as good, but the basic lines will be the same.

• Pants and skirts, I've noticed, tend to change fashion silhouette every other season, but it's a rare sweater or blouse that goes totally out of vogue. Jackets, coats, and dresses, too, go out of style more slowly. Spend your basic fashion dollars on garments you expect to have in your closet for a while and get them in colors and good, wearable fabrics you can live with. The more a garment costs, the longer you should expect to like it.

• Buy your clothes in fabrics that are wearable in more than one season, like velvets, jerseys, corduroys, rayons, silks, and heavy cottons.

Mistake-proof Shopping

To err is human, especially when it comes to buying clothes. I've spent countless dollars on styles I soon discovered I couldn't wear, because for one reason or another, they just weren't Barbara. Below are the mistake-proof tips for shopping I learned the hard way.

1. Bring a Fashion-savvy Friend With You

If you can persuade a friend with a good fashion sense to accompany you on shopping trips, you will get the benefit of her discerning eye for clothes. She should be able to tell you honestly whether the clothes you're trying on do the most for you, and to suggest separate combinations and accessories that really work. Sometimes that savvy friend is a special man. (The person who helped me develop my fashion sense was my father.) Though what you buy should please number one first, if the man in your life or your friends don't like your new costume, chances are you soon won't like it yourself.

2. Know Your Fashion Weaknesses

You may buy too many dressy clothes that go out of style before you get a chance to wear them, or too many styles that don't look well on you, or pants that are too tight. My weakness is shoes that look beautiful in the store but hurt my feet when I wear them. Know thyself. If you have your weaknesses clearly in mind, you will not be so tempted to repeat past mistakes.

3. Don't Buy Something Because It Looked Great on Someone Else

Once I bought a fabulous ruffled silk blouse in three different colors because I saw it on a friend and thought it looked perfect on her. A few wearings later I knew that ruffles were not and had never been for me. It is important to remember that your friends, the models in fashion magazines, or the stunning salesgirl are not *you*. Other people's fashion images should not dictate your own. Who are *you* and what is *your* real fashion image? These basic questions may take years of self-analysis and experimentation with different styles to answer.

Never-Never Number Two

Never buy anything without taking the time to try it on carefully. Don't let your ideas about fashion or your determination to wear a certain style obscure your vision when you look in the mirror. Examine the garment from all angles—front, back, and sides, up close and from a distance. Ask yourself if the color, fit, and line make you feel elegant and confident. Ask yourself if the mood of the garment is right for the place you're planning to wear it. If you have to ask yourself three times if the garment looks good, if you need it, if you want it, or beg the salesgirl for a positive opinion, it is probably not for you.

4. Avoid Last-minute Shopping

If you need a special dress for a special event, give yourself adequate time to shop. Waiting until the last minute may net you a desperation dress you'll wear once—uncomfortably—then shove to the back of your closet. Smart shoppers make regular rounds of their favorite stores and buy a "perfect" garment when they see it.

Never-Never Number Three

Never buy something for its price. I know ladies who won't touch a garment unless the number on the price tag is in outer space somewhere, and others who won't buy anything that's not on sale. The price has little to do with the way the garment looks on you.

5. Don't Buy a Garment That Doesn't Go With Anything You Own

The skirt may be lovely, but if you have to buy a new belt, shoes, and blouse to go with it, it's not for you. Too many unrelated items create an unwieldy, unwearable wardrobe. When you buy something new, mentally combine it with other clothes and accessories; see the complete costume in your mind's eye.

TENDER LOVING CLOTHES CARE

I'm a fanatical enemy of wrinkles, hanging threads, and ugly stains. I really believe in an old-fashioned, well-groomed appearance. Though other people may not focus directly on an untidy flaw, they will register it subconsciously and think of you as a messy, disorganized person (an image that never did anything for anybody). The state of your clothes is just as important as the style. If a garment drops a button or a hem or splits a seam, mend it before you hang it back in your closet. Otherwise you'll forget it needs repair until the rushed moment you want to put it on again. The same goes for clothes that are soiled.

Relating to Your Dry Cleaner

I send so many garments so often to my extra-special dry cleaner in L.A. that the grateful owner sends me a plant on my birthday! A good cleaning establishment like mine . . .

1. Handles clothes carefully, hanging and folding them neatly on hangers, and pads them with tissue so they won't wrinkle before you get them home.
2. Hand presses when necessary.
3. Never fades the color of clothes.
4. Blocks knit garments back to their original shape and size.

When you take a garment to the cleaner, always point out the stains you want removed. Tell him what they are and how long they've been there. Coin-operated dry cleaners do the same basic job as the others, but you will have to cope with stain removal and pressing yourself.

Stain-removing Secrets

Many stains can be removed from garments at home, especially if they are superficial and have not penetrated both sides of the fabric.

• If the garment is stained with grease, you can drench the stained area with dry-cleaning fluid, or place a plain, brown paper bag both under and over the stain and iron until the paper absorbs it. Wax can be removed with the paper-iron method, too.

• If the garment is stained with alcohol, soak it in club soda. When dry, rub white vinegar on the stain, then rinse with water.

• If a cotton, linen, or washable synthetic garment is stained with cosmetics or grass, soak it in a mixture of four tablespoons of ammonia and one quart of water, then launder as usual. Use dry-cleaning fluid on silk or wool.

• If a washable garment is stained with ink, saturate the stain with spot remover and soak in detergent and warm water. Rinse with cold water.

Never-Never Number Four

Never rub a stain, soak it in hot water, or iron it before you attempt to remove it with the correct procedure. Heat sets stains.

Laundering

The labels in most fine garments specify "dry clean only," but in many cases these DCO's can be home laundered with minimal risk if you have the time. Here's how:

• Silk can almost always be washed by hand in cold water and with a mild soap (like the kind used to wash babies' diapers). Silk actually benefits from hand-washing, because dry-cleaning fluids eventually deteriorate the fabric. Some silks are not colorfast. If you have doubts, soak a Q-Tip cotton swab in rubbing alcohol and test the fabric on an inside seam. If the color comes off on the Q-Tip, have the garment cleaned professionally.

• All wool sweaters, scarves, and even skirts can be washed by hand, and will smell fresher than when they are dry cleaned. Use a cold-water soap, squeeze suds gently through the garment, rinse in cold water, and roll in a large towel. Never squeeze or wring wool. Reshape the garment to its original size and dry on a flat surface.

• Delicate cottons can be hand laundered with a gentle soap and in lukewarm water. If you have a white blouse with colored embroidery, two tablespoons of white vinegar added to cold water will brighten the colors of the embroidery without fading it.

• All linens can be hand laundered in cold or lukewarm water with a mild soap. If you suspect the color might run, check a seam with a Q-Tip and alcohol.

• Polyester, acrylic, spandex, and most nylons are machine washable. Polyester should be dried at a low temperature, and acetates, acrylics, nylons, and spandex, should be air-dried. Rayons usually specify "dry clean only" on the label. You can generally launder them in cold water with a mild soap anyway. Dry flat.

Never-Never Number Five

Never try to hand wash velvet or jersey-type fabrics that specify "dry clean only." If you can afford it, get all pants professionally cleaned even if they are made of washable fabrics. Cleaning helps them hold their shape longer.

Bleaching

Oxygen bleaches are safe to use on all fabrics. Chlorine bleach may cause damage and may fade the colors of even light clothing. No bleach is really very kind to fabric.

Ironing

Always set your iron on the coolest temperature that will effectively press a fabric to avoid scorching and puckering. Linens, rayons, silks, and wools should be ironed on the wrong sides to prevent shine. Wools, cottons, and linens should be ironed when damp. Try putting a damp cloth between your iron and the fabric to press resistant wrinkles out of a wool garment.

Storing Clothes

Clothes should be hung on soft, padded hangers because wire hangers poke garments out of shape. I always fold my collection of knits and sweaters instead of hanging them. In the warm months, wool garments must be stored in airtight plastic containers and protected against flying munchers with mothballs.

Leather Care

Leather items are now outrageously expensive, and you will want to give good shoes and purses the longest life possible with proper care.

• Mink oil, rubbed into smooth leathers with a soft cloth, will help make them water- and stain-resistant. Let the mink oil dry overnight, then polish. (Neutral wax polish is best for purses.)

• Leather goods can be cleaned with saddle soap and water.

• Rub snakeskins with mineral oil to heighten their shine.

• Different shoe polishes have different purposes. Cream polishes soften leather, waxes give it a high shine and protection, and liquids conceal leather scars and scuffs.

• Suede should be brushed and cleaned with a special suede dry-cleaning fluid. Suede can also be cleaned with a gum eraser. (Note: Suede shoes and purses are not good investments for everyday wear. Suede is a delicate leather and will shortly look dirty and scuffed. The longest-lasting purse is one made out of a thick, shiny, dark-colored leather that doesn't scratch easily.)

• If a leather item gets wet, stuff it with paper and let it dry in a cool spot (not next to a stove, fireplace, or radiator). When dry, oil and polish.

• Store shoes and purses in soft cloth bags. When you aren't using them, stuff them with paper to preserve their shape.

THE WARDROBE MAKEOVER

Most of us have a bursting closetful of clothes, but we don't make the most of them. When we get bored with our look, we rush out to buy something new instead of considering ways to recombine, accessorize, and update the clothes we have into a series of different and exciting costumes. The following Wardrobe Makeover will tell you how:

Step 1

First, analyze your wardrobe. This will take some time. Set aside an afternoon or an evening and systematically empty your closet and drawers. Make three piles of clothing (including bathing suits and lingerie)—the clothes you always wear, the clothes you sometimes wear, and the clothes you never wear at all. These "Always," "Sometimes," and "Never" piles should tell you a lot about your real fashion image. Ask yourself why you wear the clothes you do. Undoubtedly they make you feel comfortable and attractive and perfectly suit your life-style. Are the clothes in the "Sometimes" pile there because you reserve them for special occasions, or because you don't have much to wear with them? Your "Never" pile should give you a clue about your shopping mistakes; I hope it's small. Take each garment from this pile and ask yourself why you don't like it, why you bought it, why it doesn't work, and if there's any way it can be salvaged.

Step 2

Now for a major try-on session. Try on each garment in each pile and look at yourself in the mirror as if you'd never seen yourself wearing it before. Ask yourself the following questions:

• Does it fit? In what way could it be altered to make it fit better? (Some clothes need alterations because you've gained or lost weight.)

• Does it need cleaning or repairs?

• Is it in or out of style? Is there any way it could be updated by alterations? (Note: Pants can be shortened and tapered, or cut off to make slim culottes or even shorts. The length of skirts and dresses can be changed.)

• Does this garment represent the fashion image I want for myself? (This is a more difficult, abstract question.)

Now redivide your clothes into different groups—those which need no work or changes, those which need mending, alterations, or cleaning, and those that are hopelessly out of date or simply no longer you. Plan to donate these to a worthy cause.

(They can also be exchanged with a friend for clothes in her "Hopeless" pile, which may be exactly right for you.) The hopeless garments may also be recycled, as you will see below.

Step 3

Once you've completed your basic wardrobe analysis, you will now want to consider ways to bring new life to old clothes. You can recombine and accessorize them to create exciting new outfits. Small purchases can update or add pizzazz to reliable standbys, putting a "sometimes" worn garment into the mainstream of your wardrobe. Some specific suggestions:

Recombine Colors and Silhouettes

Have you always worn your black skirt with your maroon sweater, or your plaid pants with a white blouse tucked in at the waist? One of the reasons we become bored with clothes is because we always wear them in the same ways. Once you have your wardrobe spread out in front of you, new combinations should suggest themselves. Try:

• Combining colors you never dreamed of wearing together. If you have a printed skirt or pants, and have always worn it with a blouse that perfectly matches one of the colors in the print, try combining it with a top of a different color, one that *blends* with all the colors in the print but matches none. For example, I have a blue, beige, and rust plaid skirt which I wear with a soft yellow blouse. The yellow blouse doesn't "match" any of the colors in the skirt, but blends with all of them and enhances the impact of the plaid. "Matching" is a boring word, in my opinion. Try unusual combinations. Sometimes we make intellectual decisions about color (such as, red and orange do not go), which can be reversed when we actually open our eyes and look at certain shades of those colors together.

• Recombining clothes into new silhouettes. An old, too-short dress may make an attractive tunic top. If you've always tucked your blouse in, try wearing it out and belted. You can wear different sweaters with different skirts. Try a V-necked sweater or vest over a dress. Wear jackets with garments you've never worn them with before. You may put some of the clothes in your "Never" pile back into action this way.

HERITAGE SECRETS

Caribbean Colors

In the Caribbean islands the ladies look like beautiful flowers; they wear vivid, exciting colors which bring out the glow in their dark skins. If you want to try the Caribbean way with color, wear a bright, printed-cotton skirt with a blouse in a totally different colorful print. You can also buy separates in the same printed pattern but different shades. To top off your Caribbean costume, wrap your head in a turban of yet another print or in a bright, contrasting hue.

These no-go wild prints definitely don't "match" by conservative American standards, but who cares? Look in the mirror, lovely lady; they look wonderful on *you!*

• Not every garment has to be worn the way it was intended. Nightgowns can make glamorous at-home wear. Beachwear can be transformed into party clothes. A lacy camisole makes a pretty summer blouse, and silk pajama tops make unusual shirts. A blouse can be worn as a jacket.

• Try combining separates that have different moods—dressy skirts and pants with sporty tops and vice versa. A white sweatshirt with a rhinestone pin may totally change the meaning of a businesslike skirt and take it places it wouldn't go before. Your most beautiful blouse will make a pair of jeans into party wear. Ballet slippers or sandals will turn an elegant silk dress into a down-to-earth affair.

Preselect Your Costumes

A practical way to organize your wardrobe is to preselect perfect costumes for different occasions. Take the time to preplan the look you will need for the different roles you play in life. Put together the elements of a romantic mood costume, an efficient, job-getting costume, a chic costume for outdoor wear, and a disco-dancing costume with sparkling allure. If you work in an office, you can save precious getting-out-of-the-house time in the morning by assembling five basic business outfits. Once you have the components of each clearly listed in your mind, you can dress in a flash without stopping to ponder what blouse goes with your skirt.

Recycle Clothes

The garments in your "Sometimes" or "Never" pile may be there for superficial reasons. There are many easy ways to recycle and add new interest to garments you dislike. For example:

• Change the buttons. Cheap or unattractive buttons can bring down an entire garment. Interesting buttons can be found on old clothes in thrift shops and antique stores. Mother-of-pearl, carved, or rhinestone buttons will all add flair to a garment.

• Dyeing is not an impossible art. White or beige garments can be redyed vivid colors in a washing machine. Get a book on tie dyeing or batiking, and practice your new art on T-shirts and scarves.

• If the hemstitching shows on an inexpensive dress or skirt, redo the hem by hand. This subtle touch will improve the entire look of the garment. If you have any skill at sewing, collars and sleeves can easily be converted into more attractive styles.

• Sequins, feathers, pearls, rhinestones, beads, and fancy trims can be added to jeans, shirts, sweaters, and skirts that have grown dull with time.

Change the Look of Your Clothes With Accessories

Interesting accessories wake up a tired garment. To use them effectively, envision your basic outfit, then ask yourself what splash of color, contrast in texture, or novel idea would add excitement, emphasize the mood of the costume, and pull its lines together. Study fashion magazine layouts and notice the specific ways professional stylists use belts, hats, bags, jewelry, and hose. Make a list of accessories you think will work with more than one outfit, then shop for them.

FOOTWEAR

The mood of a conservative blouse and skirt can be reversed with a pair of vivid aqua or rose stockings or little white socks.

Glittery hose peeking out of the cuffs of plain slacks add a provocative touch. Footwear can be witty, sophisticated, or outrageous, and add an interesting texture factor to your costume. Experiment!

HATS

Sometimes I put on a simple cotton slacks-and-shirt outfit, then add a little straw fedora. *Voom!* I have a sophisticated costume. I've also learned I can change a basic daytime dress into a nighttime outfit simply by adding an elegant black hat. I never wear a hat the way it's supposed to be worn but pushed backward, forward, or cocked to the side. Hats can make a costume (and a face) mysterious, important, or cute, depending on the hat.

BELTS

A belt can unify separates, add color to a neutral outfit, or dramatize a plain dress. You can wrap and double-wrap your waist with scarves, strips of fabric, men's neckties, ropes and cords, and thin pieces of leather. Invest in a special, significant belt and wear it as your trademark. Try belts in colors that contrast with the rest of your clothes.

HERITAGE SECRETS

Senegalese Bead Belt

In Senegal (and other African countries, too) many women wear a string of *Ferre* beads, made of pearl or glass, around their waists and beneath their clothes. The waist beads are not only decorative but make a musical sound when the ladies walk. The belts also create a sensual friction between two bodies engaged in making love. You can make your own Senegalese belt by stringing some pretty beads on a waist-size strand, or by adapting one of your beaded necklaces for body wear. You can wear your bead belt outside your clothes, or inside as the Senegalese do, or as a pretty accessory for your bikini.

PURSES

A purse can also emphasize the mood of your outfit and enhance its overall look. A well-shaped purse of the finest leather is an important investment for anyone who wears business clothes; a good purse shouts "classy" and "efficient," and it will wear well. My favorite purses are old alligator bags, which are now seldom made for conservation reasons. I picked up these endangered species for a few dollars at the Salvation Army, then had them repaired and reconditioned into gorgeous collectors' items. You can also make and design your own purses from interesting pieces of fabric, or substitute a basket from Africa or South America for a purse.

SCARVES, STOLES, WRAPS, ETC.

Any large piece of unusual fabric can be transformed into a stole or scarf and wrapped around the body or head.

Try sewing four silk scarves together for a multicolored stole, or wearing a bright, ethnic-looking shawl or poncho over a neutral-colored coat. If you knit or crochet, you can make shawls in your favorite color tones, too. If the color of a dress or blouse does nothing for your complexion, try adding a scarf in a flattering shade at the neckline. You can also use stoles to change the silhouette of a basic dress by wrapping them around your waist and shoulders in dramatic styles.

HERITAGE SECRETS

Mali Shawl

The Mali women of Africa make a simple but dramatic shawl by throwing a long, wide piece of brightly printed fabric over their shoulders. These shawls can also be transformed into sacks to carry things. You can create your own Mali shawl by buying a long, wide piece of brightly printed batik fabric, hemming it on all sides, and simply letting it trail carelessly over one shoulder. Your Mali shawl will add a touch of African drama to a plain cotton dress; when it gets chilly, transform the shawl into a cape or stole by wrapping it around your head and shoulders.

HERITAGE SECRETS

The African Wrap

All over Africa, women know how to make a skirt or dress from a single piece of fabric. They wrap a bright piece of cloth around their waist or chest, tuck it in, and presto! they have a comfortable, unsewn skirt that moves fluidly with the body. You can make an African wrap of your own. Simply take a piece of fabric (about two and a half yards long and thirty to forty inches wide) and place it around your waist, holding the two free ends of the fabric in front of your body with both hands. Take the left side and bring it over your stomach. (You can fold pleats into it to leave you room to walk.) Then take the part of the fabric that is still in your right hand, bring it across your stomach and tuck it securely into your waist at the left side. (This is something like wrapping a towel around yourself.) You can experiment with the wrap technique to create different styles, and pin the cloth if you're afraid it might slip. In Bali, where our beautiful, dark-skinned sisters wear a wrap skirt called a *kamben,* this sarong-like garment is secured by a bright-colored sash. (You can substitute a pretty silk scarf.) You can also wrap and tuck the fabric around your chest for a longer, elegant dress. The material you use can be a printed cotton batik, imported from Africa, India, or Indonesia, silk, or even a soft, fluid, crushed velvet or matte jersey. Wear your wrap skirt with a halter, T-shirt, camisole, or long cotton blouse. *(Note:* Wraps make excellent traveling companions because they fold into a flat, smooth package.)

JEWELRY

Jewelry is the most misused accessory. Too many ladies just toss it on without coordinating it with the rest of their costume. People should see your jewelry as an integral part of what you're wearing. Be sure that earrings, necklaces, bracelets, and rings complement not only your total look but each other, too, in material, color, and design. If you have a fabulous family heirloom, gorgeous diamond, or marvelous piece acquired on a foreign trip, design a special neutral outfit that will really show it off. If boldness is your style, emphasize it with jewelry—wear all your special rings or necklaces at once, or invest in some "fun" jewels like old rhinestones. Personally I don't wear any jewelry at all—that's *my* style.

HERITAGE SECRETS

The African Way With Jewels

African tribal women wear their wealth in the form of jewelry. Rows and rows of beautiful beads and an armload of bracelets are a beautiful woman's trademark and her bank account. If you want to experiment with the African bejeweled style, try buying and wearing more than one of everything. Your jewels don't have to be expensive. Eight vividly colored plastic bangles (they can be copper or silver, too), and rows and rows of interesting beads (try stringing your own), mixed with a copper or silver chain, and two slim hoops of gold through the ears will add an exotic flair to your party costume.

FIGURE FIXIN'

No doubt about it, an in-shape figure can carry "in" fashions with grace and flair. A trim, compact body with a flat abdomen and supple muscles not only looks good in clothes, but feels good, too. A slim, strong body is filled with energy, is less inclined to suffer freak accidents, aches, and pains, and looks younger longer.

By now most of us have heard over and again that the way to fix our figures is to maintain a nutritious, low-calorie diet and to take some form of exercise at least three times a week. There are innumerable books on the subject of diet and exercise by experts far better versed in these subjects than I. If you know nothing about physical fitness or nutrition, I suggest you check them out in the library or a bookstore as soon as possible. Meanwhile, here are a few, down-to-earth basic pointers to help you get and keep a good-looking figure—in or out of clothes.

THE NO-NONSENSE NO's FOR STAYING THIN

Take it from the lady who once made it her sacred duty to sample a chocolate mousse in every restaurant in America—*nothing* is harder than eliminating delicious treats from our diet, even when we know they make us fat. Staying slender when we are surrounded by fattening foods of every description and variety means saying a loud, inner No to many delicious calories much of the time. The older you get, the less food your body needs to maintain its ideal weight, and the louder and firmer and more often you must pronounce that negative syllable. Often devastating numbers of calories are hidden in foods we thought of as nonfattening or healthy. Below is a list of No foods and the places they hide in.

Say No to Sugar

White, refined sugar lacks vitamins, minerals, and fiber—in fact, anything worth putting into your system—and is stored in the body as fat. Sugar promotes obesity and tooth decay, and some nutritionists are convinced it also causes serious diseases. While sugary foods seem to give you a "lift" right after you eat them, they shortly deplete your energy because of the way they are metabolized. Sweets are also addictive; the more you eat, the more you want. As a former sugar addict, I can attest that my health and energy level improved enormously when I renounced sweet foods upon the recommendation of a nutritionist. Natural sweeteners, like honey and molasses, contain some minerals, but they are still sugar and still make you fat. Raw sugar and brown sugar are no better for you than white sugar. Sugar is often hidden in foods that don't really taste sweet, like canned vegetables and soups. Breakfast cereals, sodas, juices (including some that say "no sugar added"), jams, and fruit-flavored yogurts are all sugar-loaded and all fattening. Try satisfying your sweet tooth with fresh fruit (go easy, though; too much fruit is fattening also) and cutting the amount of sugar in recipes by half.

Say No to Refined Carbohydrates

Breads, pastas, and any baked goods made with white, refined flour and white rice are "empty" calories because they lack the fibers, vitamins, and minerals of natural grains and foods made with them. These refined carbohydrates (usually slathered with butter and fattening sauces to give them the taste they lack) also end up in the body as fat. You do need carbohydrates to give you energy, but try exchanging the pallid, refined versions for natural brown rice, grains, whole grain breads, whole wheat pastas, potatoes, and beans. You will find these natural carbohydrates more filling and satisfying once you get used to them. Your body will also digest them in a way that provides you with your maximum energy quotient. Alcohol, by the way, is another useless carbohydrate which turns straight into fat. Reducing your consumption of alcohol will always reduce your weight.

Say No to Excess Fats

We all need a bit of fat in our diets—but no more or less than one tablespoon of an unrefined vegetable oil every day. Most of us, however, consume much more fat than that, and fat, in any form, is absolutely loaded with calories. Too much fat in your diet not only makes *you* fat, but can cause serious diseases of the heart and arteries. Researchers now believe that excess fat also causes some forms of cancer. Fats are hiding in beef and pork, salad dressings (one hundred walloping calories per tablespoon; try my favorite substitute, plain tomato juice, instead), rich cheeses (like cream cheese, cheddar, and most French cheeses), milk, cream, butter, baked goods containing shortening or butter, granolas, seeds, nut butters, avocados, and mayonnaise. (Have I covered *everything* you really like to eat?) The easiest way to lose weight is to substitute low-fat fish and meat (like chicken minus its skin and veal), low-fat breads (like pita bread or Swedish flat breads), *tofu* and vegetables, plain yogurt, buttermilk, skim milk, cottage cheese, and mozzarella for fat-rich, caloric foods. My favorite emergency diet food is a plain baked potato elegantly served on a pretty plate. Believe it or not, the basic potato tastes terrific all by itself.

Say No to Foods Prepared in Fattening Ways

Sorry, any food that is fried or prepared in a rich sauce or gravy is automatically fattening.

Say No to Salt

Salt, nutritionists say, causes high-blood pressure in 20 percent of the population. It also helps your body retain water, which adds soggy, liquid pounds. Salt is hidden in an enormous number of canned and prepared foods, and is used as a preservative. (Any preservative beginning with the word "sodium" is a form of salt.) Condiments like mustards and soy sauce are also salty. Restaurant foods, too, are usually oversalted. This unhealthy substance is difficult to avoid. Cut the salt in recipes by a half or a third, and substitute lemon juice, spices, and herbs when possible.

Say No to Caffeine

Caffeinated beverages, like black coffee, tea, and sugarless colas, will not make you fat but they may give you the shakes, or insomnia, or make you feel hungry and empty because of the way they are metabolized in the body. Today some researchers believe that excess caffeine may cause breast cancer. Caffeine, I believe, also clouds the skin. Try substituting Postum, decaffeinated coffee, herbal teas, and mineral water with lime for nerve-jangling caffeinated beverages.

Say No to Huge Quantities of Anything

Any food is fattening if you eat large quantities of it, with the exception of raw or steamed vegetables without an oily dressing. Just because a food is "natural" or a "health food" does not mean it is necessarily slimming fare.

Never-Never Number Six

Never try to make your diet a totally joyless affair. Food is one of the great pleasures of life, and we should eat not only to become skinny, healthy biological specimens, but to delight ourselves. No one in her right mind can or should say No to all the abovementioned foods all the time, but a serious policy of restraint and moderation will reduce your weight, improve your energy level and health, and help you participate in many of life's joys.

Never-Never Number Seven

Never make a crash diet, based on a limited number of foods, a constant way of life. A good reducing diet should include a variety of different foods in small quantities; otherwise it is deficient in vitamins, minerals, and fuels your body needs to keep it in good working order. You may lose weight with a crash diet, but you will end up feeling so deprived you will be sure to overeat and gain the weight back when the diet is over. As you get older, a crash diet, which causes you to lose too much weight too quickly, may leave sags and bags in your skin as well as wrinkles.

Barbara's "Too Busy to Exercise" Exercise System

The ideal exercise program should include a vigorous aerobic exercise like running, swimming, jumping rope, tennis, squash, or paddle ball. These strengthen the muscles of the heart and lungs and improve the circulation. An exercise which stretches the muscles of the body also gives the body shape—some form of calisthenics, yoga, weight lifting, modern dance, or ballet is ideal. To really stay fit, you should do both an aerobic and a calisthenic exercise. Regular exercise is your figure's war against time—it keeps your body firm, smooth, and supple. Exercise also burns extra calories not only while you're doing it, but later, too. Experts believe that the body's metabolism is stepped up for as long as six or seven hours after you exercise. Exercise is also an excellent tension calmer—and most modern women have more than their share of *that*.

Now, I would love to be able to jog, take a yoga class, or swim regularly, but the truth is, I can't. There simply aren't enough hours in any day for me to take care of my house, myself, run a busy, demanding business, *and* carve out enough time in my life for special exercise sessions, too. Because I'm well aware of the importance of exercise, however, I've learned to incorporate it into my everyday routine. Here's how you can do it, too.

1. Walk Whenever You Can

Walking, like jogging, helps keep your weight down, strengthens leg muscles and bones, and reduces blood pressure and tension. You don't need any special walking clothes (except a comfortable pair of shoes) or a special place to walk. A brisk three-mile walk burns at least two hundred calories, and shorter walks step up your metabolism and improve your spirits and circulation. In Los Angeles I see everybody riding when they could be walking, wasting gas without wasting a single calorie. Try walking to work (it may take an extra half hour, no more), walking to the supermarket (carrying a bundle improves the effect of walking), or walking to get the newspaper. I walk with my dog, Charlie Brown, in the steep hills where I live, and run and play ball with him, too—a real workout!

2. Kitchen Calisthenics

Put on some fast music while you clean, and dance your way vigorously through chores, exaggerating your movements and stretching your body as much as possible. When you mop or sweep, *reach* with the mop or broom. Reach to the other side of the bed to tuck in the sheet instead of walking around. I always scrub the floor myself on my hands and knees even though I have a housekeeper, because it's one of the best workouts. Gardening—clipping, digging, and mowing—is also one of my favorite ways to get some exercise.

3. Reach, Stretch, and Bend Your Way Through the Day

Every morning before I get out of bed, I reach for one end of the bed with my head and arms and the other with my feet—stretching myself out, just like a rubber band. I've found that many of my everyday activities ask me to reach, stretch, or bend, and I use these simple actions to shape my figure. I keep my stepladder in the garage so I won't be tempted to use it; instead I stand on my tiptoes, stretch up my arms, and reach for things over my head. Whenever you reach up or out, hold your stomach muscles in tightly, pulling them in toward your back and up toward your chest at the same time. Keep your back as straight as possible. When you bend from the waist to pick something up, keep your legs straight and lower your back slowly, vertebra by vertebra. Hang over your feet for a minute, pick up the object, then rise back up slowly, the same way you went down. This will stretch out the muscles in your lower back and in the backs of your legs. When you squat, keep your back straight and tighten your stomach muscles.

4. Practice Invisible Exercises

When I'm sitting in a restaurant, I push up on my toes (or stand on my tiptoes while sitting down) and extend my foot, revolving it at the ankle. This secret exercise helps keep my calf, foot, and ankle muscles limber. When I'm sitting at my desk in the office, I press the small of my back against the back of the chair, then try to push my stomach back to meet it. This contracts the stomach muscles, making them stronger. While I'm driving, I relax tense muscles in my shoulders by bringing the shoulders up toward my ears, then lowering them back and down at every stoplight. Then I reverse the action, raising my shoulders up to my ears, then squeezing them down and together in the front. I also do head rolls whenever I can, stretching my right ear straight down toward my shoulder, reaching back with my head, and then stretching my left ear down toward my left shoulder. No one sees these exercises, but they help me keep in shape.

HERITAGE SECRETS

Posture Improvement

The most expensive, well-designed outfit in the world will look like a flour sack on a slouching figure. A truly elegant posture, a straight back, and a head held high, on the other hand, will transform even a flour sack into a designer creation. Women in African and Asian countries have regal bearing which makes their often simple clothes look like queenly robes. Why? Because from childhood they carry heavy loads on their head, which strengthen their neck muscles and force them to stand up straight. To improve your posture, try the old trick of walking with a book on your head. Then add more books, until you, too, can carry a heavy load gracefully.

Bring Back the Girdle!

Girdles have been "out" for years, and I, for one, would welcome this trusty figure-shaper back in. Though we all know we should slim and firm our torsos with proper diet and exercise, many of us stubbornly continue to indulge our taste buds and sedentary habits and firmly believe a few extra pounds are voluptuous. If you ask me, a little extra flesh is only a problem when it jiggles around in clothes. If anything below your waist wiggles when you walk, no fitted garment will look attractive. A good foundation can help you package your extra pounds smoothly and should be part of your regular grooming preparations. Try on girdles as you would shoes until you find a lightweight style that's reasonably comfortable.

Perfecting Your Figure With Illusion

Clothes give your figure grace and mystery, and reveal its interesting contours by slightly disguising them. Everybody's figure has flaws which can be softened and concealed with the right clothing silhouette. The lines of a style can change the relationship of one part of your body to another, and fill and trim places that need filling and trimming. Below are some suggestions on how to use clothes to revise your figure.

If Your Body Is Too Big . . .

Any part of your body that's big will look larger if the garment you choose to cover it is too tight or too voluminous. Frills and ruffles, large vivid prints, heavy, coarse, or extremely textured fabrics, shiny fabrics, bold, horizontal stripes and plaids will also make the large look even larger. If your figure is ample or big-boned, the keys to minimizing it are to . . .

• Wear well-tailored dresses, skirts, and pants with vertical, fluid lines. Your clothes should fall loosely and smoothly, yet fit very well. Pants and skirts should fit easily in the stomach area and have some fullness in the seat. Avoid pleats and gathers at the waist.

• Choose single color tones (not necessarily drab or conservative ones), or small, discreet prints and plaids.

• Keep your accessories moderate in size. Huge purses and wide belts will emphasize the impression of bigness.

• If any one part of your body is large, deemphasize it by making the part above or below it fuller. A large bosom seems smaller when you wear an A-line, a pleated, or a flared skirt that fills out the hip area. If you wear a slim, straight skirt, you emphasize the difference in proportion between the top and the

bottom of your body. If your hips are too wide, wear loose skirts,
sweaters, or overblouses; these will minimize the contrast between your hips and your bust. Hats and scarves wrapped around
the head or neck will also help balance the large-hipped figure.

• Avoid skirts and jackets that are too short. These will make
heavy arms and legs look bunchy.

If Your Body Is Thin . . .

If any part of your body is too thin, don't cover it with a
skintight garment or leave it bare. Clothes that are tailored fairly
close to the body, but not too close, will make you look
fashionably thin instead of starvation slender. Pleats and gathers
are also becoming.

• Exotic prints, wide stripes, plaids, and glittery or shiny
fabrics will fill out a thin body. You can also wear nubby or thick-
woven wools and wide-waled corduroys. Avoid clinging materials.

• Layered outfits will add dimension to a slender figure. Try
tunics, vests, and blouses over turtlenecks and camisoles.

• Separates in contrasting colors and colorful belts and
footwear will make your body look fuller.

If Your Body Is Short . . .

Any elongated, smooth silhouette—a high or Empire waist-
line and A-line dresses and skirts—will make a short body appear
taller. Tapered pants with a pegged leg, or narrow, straight-cut
pants will make your legs look longer if they are slender. (Avoid
pants with cuffs.) The shorter the garment you wear on the top of
your body, the longer your legs will look in pants or a skirt. A hat
or a headwrap will add height, too. Avoid a cluttered look; lots of
accessories, trimmings, and frills will break up your height and
make you look shorter.

If Your Body Is Tall . . .

Fashion silhouettes are created for the tall body, and you
should be able to wear almost any style, especially if you are
slender. If you are big-boned or heavy, follow the style guidelines
for "The Big Body." If you want to minimize long legs, arms, or

neck, wear clothes that cover them with soft, flowing lines. Soft shirts with fuller sleeves and scarves and stoles will also soften angular lines. Calf-length skirts and cuffed pants will break up the line of your legs.

If Your Body Is Short-Waisted . . .

If you are short-waisted, you will look more so if you tuck your tops into your skirts and pants or wear high-waisted clothes. If you like the neat, tucked-in look, try wearing skirts and pants with waistbands that fall slightly below the line of your real waist. A blouse tucked into a slim skirt will not look as short-waisted as a blouse tucked into a full skirt. Try wearing tunics and blouses outside skirts and pants and belting them. A layered look on top will also make your waist seem longer.

Never-Never Number Eight

Never try *too* hard to camouflage a figure flaw. You may end up calling attention to it. For years I wore only strangling turtlenecks and voluminous blouses in hopes of hiding a bosom I considered too large. In fact, peoples' eyes were drawn to my chest, or, at least, to its elaborate disguises. (Who ever heard of a turtleneck in ninety-degree weather?) If you wear flat shoes to make you look shorter, or dresses that resemble tents to make you look smaller, people may not notice your height or breadth, but they will notice that you look peculiar and not as elegant as you could. Your so-called flaw may be far more devastating in your own mind than it is in the mirror. Look again! Today I'm proud of the most feminine part of my anatomy.

5

Beautiful Hands and Feet

Our hands are almost always visible, describing what we do in life, punctuating what we say, and communicating our loving feelings. Like any other part of you, your hands deserve beautifying care. Their skin should be soft, the nails polished and well-groomed. Our nails, I believe, are a special beauty asset because of the contrast they provide to the dark skin of our hands. Though your feet spend most of their life hiding in shoes, they emerge from hibernation on beaches, in sandals, and at crucial romantic moments, when they can be rough and calloused turn-offs or sensual turn-ons. They, too, need care to make them a pleasure to touch and behold.

THE ESSENTIAL MANICURE

A professional manicure is one of the world's greatest luxuries. I love relaxing in a pretty salon and daydreaming while an expert manicurist pampers my nails. A home manicure consumes less time and money, however, and can be just as effective if you follow the eight steps below.

What You Need

Choose a well-lighted spot in your home and spread the manicuring tools and ingredients listed below on a clean towel on a table before you begin. Advance preparation will save you the polish-smearing aggravation of searching for a missing tool in the middle of your manicure.

1. A nonoily polish remover and cotton;
2. An orangewood stick wrapped in cotton;
3. A cuticle-removing cream or gel;
4. A cuticle nipper;
5. A nail clipper to trim the nails;
6. An emery board;
7. A small bowl filled with water and a mild detergent;
8. A fingernail brush;
9. A clear base coat for the bottom of the nail;
10. Nail enamel (with the top of the bottle loosened);
11. A clear enamel for coating the top of the nail;
12. A glass of ice water.

Step 1: Removing Old Polish

Remove polish with a nonoily polish remover and cotton. Some manicurists recommend using an oil-based remover; this is supposedly less drying to the nails. It tends to leave an oily film on the nail, however, which prevents your polish from adhering smoothly. The nonoily remover will not dry your nails if you use it quickly and sparingly. It isn't necessary to totally drench the nail with the remover.

Step 2: Smoothing the Cuticles

Apply your cuticle-removing cream or gel to the cuticles. *Remover* is an inaccurate name for this substance; it will not actually remove the cuticle, but will soften it and make it easier to push back from the surface of the nail. Take an orangewood stick with the tip wrapped in cotton and push the cuticle back in a circular motion, moving the stick down and around. Then remove the excess cuticle that clings to the nail with cotton, or, if it is stubborn, with your cuticle nippers. You can also remove any hangnails with the nippers.

Never-Never Number One

Never start cutting your cuticles with a cuticle nipper. Though the cuticle will look smooth after your nipping job, it will rapidly grow back tougher and larger than it was before, and you will have to keep cutting it. Cutting stimulates the growth of the cuticle. Only use the nipper to remove dangling hangnails, not the firm part of the cuticle. You should also throw away the metal pusher in your manicuring kit. The cuticle is delicate, and the metal instrument may damage it and the matrix at the base of the nail behind the cuticle from which the nails grow.

Step 3: Shaping the Nails

Clip the nails with a clipper. I like the large kind made for toenails, preferably with a straight not a curved edge. Clip the top of the nail straight across, then shape it with an emery board. File the top straight across for a square-shaped nail. For an oval-shaped nail, file from left to center, then from right to center. Move the file in one direction only. Don't saw back and forth.

Never-Never Number Two

Never use a metal file on your nails. Filing back and forth with this minisaw will cause the edges of your nails to split and peel.

Step 4: Soaking and Cleaning the Nails

Now soak your nails in the bowl of water and detergent, as long as you can do so patiently. Brush the nails with a nail brush to clean them and remove excess cuticle. When you remove your nails from the solution they should be perfectly clean. To make sure, go over them lightly with cotton and a trace of the nonoily remover. Your nails must be clean and dry before you apply the polish. Once they are ready, don't even touch the surface with your own fingers, which may leave a trace of oil on the nail.

Step 5: Applying the Base Coat

Apply the clear base coat to your nails. This is a necessary step. The clear base makes the nails less porous and less liable to absorb the colored nail enamel you will apply afterward. Without the base a dark-colored polish may stain your nails over a period of time. The base smooths out tiny pits and ridges in the nail, allowing the enamel to go on smoother. The base will also protect your nail from the polish, preventing reactions should you be allergic to the enamel. By the time you finish applying the base coat to your other hand, the base coat on the first hand should be dry and you can apply the enamel.

Step 6: Applying the Enamel.

Apply the enamel with even strokes, beginning at the base of the nail and brushing it up toward the top. Remove excess drips from the brush before you begin. When you've covered the surface of the nail, turn your hand over and apply polish around the free edge of the nail along the tip. Don't continue the polish down into the inside of the nail—keep it along the edge. This step builds up an extra ridge on the nail, which makes the polish last longer without chipping. Then move on to the other hand. When the first coat is dry, apply a second coat, also adding an extra ridge of polish to the free edge of the nail.

Selecting Nail Enamel

Nail enamel is really an accessory and should be selected to blend with the colors of your outfit and your lipstick. Nail enamel should also flatter the skin tones of your hands. The color doesn't have to *match* your lipstick or clothes, but it shouldn't fight with them either. Some colors, like pale, smoky browns with a pink or plum tone, pale neutrals, platinums, or very clear reds, will blend with almost any other color you're wearing. An unusual or extravagant color—like hot pink or orange—can add an extra note of color flair to your costume. You can also try applying a darker-colored enamel over a lighter shade in the same color range, or vice versa, for a custom blend. Experiment! My manicurist does not recommend the frosted shades. They are made with a very harsh ingredient—like housepaint, she says—which eats away at the nail. If you want to wear a frosted shade, apply it *over* a nonfrosted enamel.

Never-Never Number Three

Whatever color of nail polish you choose, it won't look good if it's chipped. Nothing looks more untidy or calls more negative attention to your hands than polish that looks like a small animal has been nibbling on it. Most hands require a fresh manicure every week. In between, it takes only seconds to touch up chipped polish. If you haven't got the time to perform the necessary upkeep on long red talons, stick to a natural-colored nail. There is nothing unglamorous about a clean, pearly nail; it looks efficient, too!

Recently I was persuaded that short nails can also be attractive. My cosmetic company's insurance agent threatened to raise our coverage by thousands of dollars a year when he spotted my long red daggers on a TV show. My nails, he claimed, were potentially dangerous weapons because I touched ladies' faces with them when I applied their makeup. My shorter, lawsuit-free nails are just as pretty, and I can actually work better with them.

Step 7: Applying the Top Coat

The final coat of polish should be a clear top coat, which protects the enamel. Some ladies use the base coat for this purpose. The top-coat type of product, however, is formulated especially to seal the polish. When you apply it, again add the extra ridge to the free edge of your nail.

Step 8: Drying the Polish

Wait five minutes until the polish is almost dry then immerse your hands in a glass of ice water. The icy water magically hardens the polish and fuses the four coats you've applied together, helping them stay on longer. Dip the nails in the water, then remove them for a period of ten minutes. The ice-water technique works better than the quick-drying sprays. When your nails are dry, be sure to remove any flecks of polish from your fingers and hands. Nail polish doesn't belong on your fingers any more than lipstick belongs on your teeth.

TWO TECHNIQUES FOR EXTENDING YOUR NAILS

Long, shapely nails have always been an unmistakable symbol of glamour and sophistication, not to mention riches. In many societies of the past, only royal ladies who didn't have to do any work with their hands could afford the luxury of long fingernails. Today even a modern woman who uses her fingers in the garden, kitchen, or office can have queen-status nails with a little help from artificial substances. Nail-sculpting techniques, which construct dragon-lady talons totally from acrylic or porcelain, demand professional know-how. Below, however, are two modified techniques to extend your nails that you can do easily yourself.

A word of warning: Before you put any glue or acrylic substance on your nail, you should know that these substances are likely to make your natural nail softer because they are strong and harsh and prevent the nail from breathing. (Some people's nails are more affected by artificial nails than others.) Remember, your nails only grow about an eighth of an inch a month. If you ruin the ones you've got, it will take a long time for nature to replace them with new ones. Acrylics also make nails more susceptible to fungus infections, and some people are allergic to artificial nails. If you have an acrylic on your nail and you notice any sign of redness or swelling, remove it immediately and see a physician. (Remove the acrylic by soaking it in nail-polish remover, then chipping it off with a nail file.) I think it is best to give your nails a rest between sculpting procedures.

Quick Party-time Nail Extension

If your nails are short and you want to create a longer, sophisticated nail for a special occasion, buy some artificial tips (made of tenite acetate) and apply them as follows:

1. Clean, clip, and shape your nail as described in The Essential Manicure.

2. Buff the nail very lightly, using a special sandpaper-type buffer. These buffers look like emery boards mounted on a cushion and may be long or disc-shaped. They can be purchased in drugstores or in cosmetic-supply stores. If you can't find the special buffer, substitute a very fine sandpaper. This buffing roughens the surface of the nail, making it easier for the glue to adhere.

3. The artificial tips come in different sizes. Before you apply the glue, fit each of your nails with the appropriate-sized tip, then lay them out in the order you will use them. Apply a five-minute-type nail glue to the tips and fit them to your nail. (Don't use any other kind of glue but the one made especially for artificial nails.) Finish fitting and glueing the tips to one hand, and let the glue dry completely.

4. Trim the artificial nail to the length you like, then file it into shape with an emery board.

5. Buff the place where the artificial tip joins your real nail with your sandpaper-type buffer.

6. Now do the other hand.

7. Apply a ridge-filler-type base to your nails. This special base coat will even out the difference between your real nail and the artificial nail.

8. Polish with enamel as described in The Essential Manicure.

Note: Your artificial tips will last no more than a couple of days (unless you are very careful to protect them) and will dissolve when you remove the polish with polish remover.

Easy Nail Sculpture

For an artificial nail that will last at least two weeks and is relatively easy to sculpt, follow the procedure below:

1. Buy both a package of artificial nail tips and an acrylic nail-sculpting kit. (The price of the two kits is modest—far less than having your nails professionally sculpted.)

2. Clean and prepare the nail as described in The Essential Manicure.

3. Apply the artificial tips to one hand, using the special glue, then trim and file them to the shape you desire (as in the directions above). Buff the nail with the sandpaper-type buffer.

4. Now apply the acrylic substance, mixing it as directed on the package. You will not be using the silver wings (included in the package) to sculpt acrylic tips that extend beyond the edge of your own nails. This involves a great deal of skill and practice. Instead the artificial tips will form a base for the acrylic. Apply the acrylic substance to the entire nail, including the tip, with a brush. (A small, sable water-color brush is perfect.) Let the acrylic spread by itself for a second or two. It will become a gel and tend to take the shape of your nail. Then, while the acrylic is still soft, work it over the nail with your brush. It may be necessary to add more of the acrylic to completely cover the nail and the tip. Spread and smooth it.

5. Wait until the acrylic is dry (it will sound like glass when you tap it with a hard object), then file down the excess with a steel file until the artificial nail looks as smooth as a real one. Then buff with the sandpaper-type buffer.

6. Do the other hand.

7. Polish with a ridge-filler base and enamel.

Note: This entire process takes about two hours. When your own nail starts to grow, it will push a space between the acrylic nail and your cuticle. You will want to fill this space with another application of acrylic, and smooth the place where the new acrylic joins the old with a file before polishing.

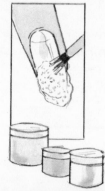
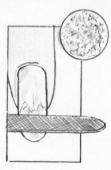

Wrappin' n' Cappin'

If your own nails are long, you may simply want to cap them with an acrylic substance without adding the additional tip. The acrylic cap will protect the shape of the nail and keep it from breaking (though continual capping will tend to make nails soft, as stated above). A process in which your nails are "wrapped" with a thin coating of paper is a safe protection plan that will encourage your nails to grow. When the paper "wrapper" is removed, the long, strong nails underneath will be all yours. Ask your manicurist for a wrap demonstration.

LIFESAVERS FOR NAILS

Whether your natural nails are long and well-manicured or you have long, sculpted nails, you must learn to use your fingers in new ways to protect them. Try handling objects with the balls instead of the tips of your fingers, and use a pencil to dial the telephone. Don't use your nails to massage your scalp when shampooing (it's bad for the scalp and for the nails). Long nails rebel against heavy chores and lots of water. Some detergents, I've found, actually deteriorate the acrylic nail. Take extra time to put on a pair of rubber gloves, and make them the mainstay of your housecleaning wardrobe. Get outside help when doing hooks, little buttons, and jewelry with tiny clasps, and beware of "nail traps" in the form of your car ashtray, pocketbook clasps, and lids you must remove with your fingertips.

DAZZLE-TIME TOUCHES FOR NAILS

Here are some of my favorite techniques for adding a special dazzle to my nails for parties and glamorous evenings.

1. Add a sequin to the center of each nail tip with a touch of five-minute-type nail glue.

2. Now your nails can wear jewels in the form of tiny fourteen-carat gold charms which can be inserted in acrylic nails.

3. Use your artistic talent to paint moons, stripes, and wavy lines on top of your final polish with another color of enamel or with a shiny gold, silver, or frosted shade. Outrageous!

4. Add a brilliant white tip to your nails with a shimmery platinum polish. You can emphasize the white tip by using a nail-whitening pencil on the inside of your nail.

HERITAGE SECRETS

Balinese Gold Fingers

In Bali young women used to wear long shields of pure gold over their nails. These gold fingers were not only beautiful, ornamental status symbols, but helped the exotic Balinese to gesture more expressively when they did their famous ceremonial dances. To create your own version of gold fingers, spread some artificial tips with a thin coating of glue, then dip them in gold glitter. Fit them to your fingernails and leave the tips extravagantly long.

TROUBLESHOOTING

Below are a list of common nail problems along with their causes and cures.

Problem: Ridged Nails With Uneven Surfaces; Splitting, Peeling Nails

The Cause

Vertical ridges on the nails may be inherited. Sawing nails back and forth with an emery board or a metal file will aggravate a ridge condition and cause nails to peel. Nails may also peel and split if they are allergic to the polish you're using. Some so-called nail hardeners contain a very irritating ingredient—formaldehyde—which can sabotage the nail.

The Cure

File and shape nails correctly as described in The Essential Manicure. Buffing your nails regularly should also help remove the imperfections. Buy a good chamois-skin buffer that fits comfortably into your hand and buff each nail about seven seconds when you do your regular manicure. Buffing with a sandpaper-type buffer will also remove ridges. Don't buff with anything too often or you will weaken the entire nail. (See Glamicure for Troubled Nails, page 186, for an attractive way to cure the ridged condition.)

Problem: Soft Nails That Break Easily

The Cause

Both external and internal factors may weaken your nails. Submerging your hands in water or harsh detergent solutions may soften the nails, causing hangnails and ragged cuticles, too. Nails don't like water! Acrylic also softens the nails. An inadequate diet may be reflected in inadequate nails.

The Cure

Wear rubber gloves to protect your hands from water. Once a day brush your nails with a small, stiff brush and soap and water. The brushing stimulates blood circulation in the matrix, helping nails grow longer and stronger.

The Nail Diet

Your nails, like your hair, are composed of a protein substance. A high-protein diet is necessary for their well-being. If your diet is deficient in eggs, meat, or dairy products, start feeding your nails some of these important boosters now. My manicurist recommends four eggs a week to ensure strong, lustrous nails. There's no guarantee, however, that the protein you put in your body will travel straight to your nails, so don't overdo it.

The Gelatin Controversy

For years gelatin has been recommended as a potent nail-builder. Now many manicurists say that this is pure myth and fairy tale; gelatin will do little or nothing for your nails. My manicurist, Donna LeClair, swears that gelatin will improve your nails if (and get ready for a big *if*) you take five to nine capsules a day for a period of five or six months. You must take the gelatin continually and not expect to see even a trace of improvement before the six months are up.

HERITAGE SECRETS

Moroccan Henna Wrap for Problem Nails

Natural henna strengthens the hair and will also smooth and strengthen nails, as women in North Africa well know. To henna-wrap your nails the Moroccan way:

1. Mix a quarter of a package of neutral henna with a quarter cup of boiling water and add an egg for extra protein enrichment. Make sure you use a pure, neutral henna (not a red or a burgundy unless you want orange nails).
2. Brush the henna mixture on the nails of one hand with a small brush, and then wrap each nail tightly in silver foil.
3. Do the other hand.
4. Leave the henna on for ten or fifteen minutes, then wash off thoroughly.

With the leftover henna you can also do your toenails.

Glamicure for Troubled Nails

Treating the surface of the nail is one of the best ways to make it stronger. Soft, ridged, splitting, or chipping nails can be improved with the following manicure.

Step 1: Shape and clean the nail as described in The Essential Manicure.

Step 2: Buff away the imperfections on the nail surface with a sandpaper-type buffer. Then buff with your chamois-skin buffer.

Step 3: Brush on a liquid-protein treatment. The protein should be the type that can be partially absorbed by the nail.

Step 4: Apply a ridge-filler to the nail instead of your usual clear base coat. The cloudy ridge-filler smooths the nail and seals in the protein.

Step 5: Apply a clear base coat to the nail and, if you like, follow with a nail enamel. The ridge-filler will prevent the nail enamel from working into the irregularities on the surface of the nail and chipping. Consider eliminating the polish; the ridge-filler and clear base coat alone will give your nails an elegant, pearlized glow, guaranteed to blend perfectly with your dark skin tones and any lipstick or outfit you wear.

Problem: Nails Stained by Nail Enamel or Yellowish Nails

The Cause

Applying enamel without a base or contact with staining substances.

The Cure

To restore stained nails to their normal tone, add four capfuls of hydrogen peroxide to the water and detergent solution in which you soak your nails. To cure yellow nails, cut a lemon in half and stick each finger into the center for several minutes. The flesh of the lemon has a powerful bleaching agent. You can also squeeze the lemon and bathe your nails in the juice.

Problem: Ragged, Uneven, Overgrown, or Thickened Cuticles

The Cause

Cutting cuticles with a nipper or insufficient lubrication.

The Cure

Cuticles should be pushed back and lubricated every night of your life as part of your regular nail maintenance program. An especially rich hand cream, A and D ointment, or a commercial cuticle cream are all good cuticle softeners. Even if you've been nipping your cuticles and they've grown large and tough, regular push-back-and-cream treatments should eventually soften them to the point where you can quit nipping.

DREAMTIME HAND AND CUTICLE TREATMENT

Here is a fabulously effective treatment for rough and ragged cuticles, especially valuable in the winter months when cold weather conditions and indoor heating dry out your cuticles and hands:

1. Heat about a quarter of a cup of Vaseline petroleum jelly in a small pot on the stove.

2. While you're relaxing or watching television, coat your nails and hands with the softened Vaseline and let it sink in. Repeat this two or three times in the course of an evening.

3. When you've given your hands the final application of the Vaseline, cover them with a pair of white cotton gloves and let the lubricating jelly soften your hands and cuticles overnight. The Vaseline will shrink the pores of your skin and make your hands look younger and softer overnight; your cuticles, too, will become amazingly smoother.

TOUCHWORTHY HANDS

Your hands are constantly exposed to the weather as well as to harsh cleaning fluids and detergents. Without special care they will age faster than the rest of your body, or become untouchable, with dry, rough skin. Please follow my cardinal rules for hand preservation:

1. Wear rubber gloves when doing household chores and cotton work gloves when gardening.

2. Carry a bottle of mineral oil or lanolin-based hand lotion, or a tube of Vaseline or cocoa-butter-type cream in your purse, and scatter additional minisized containers of hand protection around the house (in convenient spots in the kitchen, by the telephone or TV set). Hand lotion gets washed away almost as fast as you put it on and needs to be reapplied frequently. Once is not enough.

3. Apply a sun-protection lotion containing PABA to your hands when you're out of doors to protect them from aging ultraviolet rays.

4. Always wear gloves in the cold.

BLEACHING BROWN SPOTS

Hands develop dark age spots faster than the rest of the body. These hard-to-vanquish stains may lighten if you apply a bleaching cream to the brown spots only. Castor oil, too, is reputed to bleach brown spots out of the skin. With regular application and a little luck, you may see an improvement in three to six months.

WHITE-KID HAND SMOOTHER

For a smoothing "facial" for your hands, to be applied at bedtime, select a very rich cream—the type you'd use to prevent wrinkles— and massage it into your hands. Use your thumb to press out kinks in your joints and muscles, pulling each finger with the fingers of your opposite hand. Then coat your hands, cream and all, with an extra sealer of Vaseline. Put on a pair of old white-kid gloves (found in thrift shops for pennies) and wear them to bed. The kid gloves supply a mysterious hand-smoothing ingredient, and they prevent the moisture-sealing oils in the cream and Vaseline from vanishing into the sheets or the atmosphere.

SENSUOUS FOOT CARE

Each of your feet contains twenty-six little bones—more bones than any other single part of your anatomy—dozens of ligaments, and layer after layer of muscles (four in the sole of the foot alone). These complicated structures are so well-built because they are entirely responsible for your land transportation; they trudge countless miles every year with your entire weight resting on top of them. Needless to say, your feet suffer extraordinary wear and tear, and you owe them special care and attention. Feet respond gratefully to sensuous care by becoming part of your sensuous appeal. (Men, I've discovered, are most attracted to a pretty pair of feet.)

A professional pedicure is a must if your feet have become unusually rough and calloused. Though some corns and bunions are born all by themselves—for hereditary reasons or because of the structure of the foot itself—most are your feet's way of protesting unfair shoes. These, and plantar warts, a form of virus, should be treated by a podiatrist. My Princess Pedicure below, however, will pamper your hard-walkin' feet on a regular basis and keep them pretty and soft.

The Princess Pedicure

What You Need

1. A bathtub or basin full of warm soapy water for foot-soaking, or a portable foot-care center which massages your feet with warm, swirling water.
2. Polish remover and cotton;
3. Toenail clipper;
4. Emery board;
5. Hindo stone (a long, thin pumice stone) and cuticle-removing lotion or gel;
6. A pumice stone, a scraper, or both;
7. Cotton pads;
8. Base coat, enamel, and top coat.

HERITAGE SECRETS

Japanese Foot Massage

The feet need special attention because, according to Oriental doctors, the nerves from all the organs in the body have their sensitive endings in our toes and soles. Massaging your feet the Japanese way will improve the health of your internal organs and relax feet that are exhausted from a tough day of standing or a fine night of dancing. You can massage your own feet or give this special labor of love to a friend.

1. Dig into the sole of the foot and the areas between the toes with a hooked thumb and the knuckle of your middle finger. This must be somewhat painful in order to be effective. If you're feeling nervous or tense, concentrate on the middle of the sole beneath the arch.

2. Now lubricate your feet with almond oil and work it into the tight tendons and muscles of your feet by pressing along the sole and top of the foot with your thumb. Pull each toe hard.

Step 1: Remove toenail polish with cotton and nonoily polish remover.

Step 2: Soak your feet for ten to fifteen minutes in the bathtub or basin filled with water and detergent, or in your portable foot-care center. You can add a touch of fragrant bath oil or some Epsom salts to the water if your feet are aching. When your feet have softened in the water, rub your heels and soles with the pumice stone. You can also use the metal scraper put out by foot-care product manufacturers. Never pumice or scrape too vigorously or too long. No part of your foot should bleed or feel overly tender when you are finished. Two or three strokes per area is enough, especially if you are using the sharp metal scraper. You should scrape or pumice your feet only once a week. Too much rubbing will promote rather than discourage callus formation. After you've finished, your feet should feel baby-soft. I also like to scrub my feet with a stiff brush like a bath brush to get them really clean.

Never-Never Number Four

Never use a very sharp tool called a Credo blade for home pedicures. These blades are potentially too dangerous in the hands of a nonprofessional. Please don't try to shave off corns or bunions or calluses with a razor blade either.

Step 3: Apply cuticle remover to the cuticles of the toes and use the Hindo stone to push the softened cuticles back. You can also use an orangewood stick wrapped in cotton, but never use a metal pusher.

Step 4: Clip the toenails squarely across the top with the large clipper. Then smooth the edges by filing in one direction with an emery board. Never try to shape the toenail into an oval by clipping it or filing it along the sides. This will cause the nail to turn in and grow into your foot (spelling pain and a visit to the podiatrist). The square-shaped toenail with slightly rounded corners is the best-looking and most practical shape. *(Note:* Keeping toenails clipped and smooth between pedicures will help keep snags out of your stockings.)

Step 5: Place cotton pads between your toes to separate them and polish toenails, first using a base coat, then two coats of enamel, and then a top coat as you would on your fingernails. Let toenails dry thoroughly.

BE KIND TO YOUR FEET

The best way to be kind to your feet is to choose comfortable shoes for everyday wear, and save the elegant spikes that ache, press, and squeeze for special occasions (see Chapter 5, "A Footnote About Shoes"). Your feet will also appreciate stockings or socks, especially with high-heeled shoes; hosiery provides a cushion between your sensitive sole and the ground and prevents calluses from forming. Finally, lubricate the skin of your beautiful feet regularly with a lotion when sunbathing, and don't forget to moisturize them with a rich lotion every night.

6

Star Quality: Becoming Conscious of the Total You

DEFINING THE BEAUTIFUL WOMAN

Think of a woman you consider beautiful and picture her in your mind's eye. You may see before you a famous personality, or someone you know. Now ask yourself why you think this woman is beautiful. What is it about her glamorous image you envy and want for yourself? Your answer, I predict, will be vague at first. When you picture your ideal in your imagination, you may realize there are things about her that are less than perfect (almost no one is without a flaw); yet to you, she is still beautiful. "It's *something* about her . . ." you may say, then declare that real beauty defies definition. Don't give up! If you really stop and think, you can pin down and define exactly why she is the most gorgeous person you know. It may be her lovely features, her figure, or her hair that give her that special impact, but it may also be a number of smaller, less definite attributes—her gestures, smile, voice, the obvious *care* she takes with her appearance, the way she walks, her hands, her buoyant energy, her warmth and hospitality. Everything about her physical being and personality may work together to create an harmonious impression of glamour and charm.

STAR QUALITY

A beautiful woman has what I call "Star Quality." Star Quality is not vague or intangible; it is the specific things you do to make yourself highly visible and project your entire being to the world.

When I was studying acting (and trying to develop Star Quality for professional reasons), I learned to be conscious of every single movement I made on stage. I learned that the way I lifted a glass to my lips, spoke, or gestured revealed a vital characteristic about the person I was playing to the audience. I remember spending a good two hours in acting class practicing the different ways to open and shut a door (angrily, calmly, decisively). As an actress I learned that people see and register everything you do, and everything you do communicates a definition of yourself.

Later my training in self-projection helped me communicate a specific image to the business world. When I found myself the president of my own cosmetics firm and I had to appear on television, or speak to newspaper reporters and at special luncheons held for me, I knew all eyes were watching, waiting to see how this young black woman, one of the first to break into the cosmetics industry, would behave and how she would handle herself. Then my ability to sit, move, speak with authority, and even open doors served me well.

You don't have to go to acting classes or modeling school to develop Star Quality. You can achieve the same results by simply becoming more aware of yourself, by planning the effect you want to create and not leaving the impression you make to chance. Star Quality involves becoming conscious of your skin, hair, and wardrobe—as well as your hands and feet and your posture—of the way you move, your attitude, and your surroundings. A woman with Star Quality thinks about what she does and how she does it. She considers what she wants to say and how she wants to look, and then sets about to accomplish those goals. And, of course, a true star is also well aware of the way she treats other people, the warmth and concern she expresses to them. In other words, to have Star Quality is to be self-conscious in a positive way that enables you to create the woman you want to be out of your own raw material—yourself!

Treating Yourself Like a Star

A lady with Star Quality treats herself like an important and privileged person. She knows that in order to command attention from others, she must lavish plenty of it on herself. She pampers her physical being—spending time on her face, figure, and wardrobe, as I've suggested throughout this book—but she also pampers herself in special, private ways that only she knows about.

Even when I plan to spend my evening alone, I come home from the office and put on a pretty, feminine robe or nightgown. (Believe me, I shop for every nightgown as carefully as for an expensive dress.) I set my table with my best silver and use a linen napkin, instead of a paper one. I light a candle and pour a glass of wine. Then, even my easy-to-fix hamburger and salad tastes like the finest meal in the finest restaurant. Even though I'm sitting at the table alone, I feel pampered and important and content.

Once a neighbor dropped by to borrow something and saw my table elegantly set and me wearing a special gown. "I'm sorry to interrupt you," she apologized. "I didn't know you had a guest." "Yes, I do," I said. "It's me! I'm my own guest."

What makes you feel pampered is a personal matter. For some ladies it might be squeezing fresh orange juice for themselves in the morning, or fixing a gourmet meal to eat alone at night. For others it might be buying fresh flowers for the table, or treating themselves to a professional massage. You can pamper your soul, too, with tickets to a play or concert that you attend alone. The point is there are times when you have to make yourself feel special because there is no one else willing to do it for you. Pampering yourself makes you feel good about yourself and enables you to communicate your positive self-concept to other people, who will give back positive vibrations in return.

Star Quality care also means taking time out to make sure your body benefits from regular checkups from your dentist and doctor and professional beauty services when necessary.

Star Quality Surroundings

Every room in my house is inviting; every room has a whimsical, glamorous, or romantic touch, and I worked hard to make it that way. Most of my furniture comes from antique and thrift shops. I invested some money and personal time into reupholstering and refinishing these inanimate objects to give them my personal stamp and make them part of me.

Your home reflects your habits, aesthetic taste, and personality. The places in which you spend your time, and the objects you handle every day, take on the aura you project. Therefore, the plates on which you serve your meals, the sheets on your bed, the lighting in your rooms, your furniture, and decorations, all deserve the same *self-conscious* attention as your makeup and wardrobe. Examine your rooms as you would your face in the mirror and ask yourself what *feelings* your surroundings communicate, and if they provide an accurate reflection of the person you want the world to see. If not, make a study of home decoration and learn what furnishings, color schemes, and interesting ideas will portray your personality.

Star Quality Fragrance

A woman's fragrance is her most intimate trademark, the invisible part of herself that makes a lasting impression on other people's senses. Your very personal perfume or cologne, then, should be selected with particular care; a fragrance should put a subtle exclamation point on your total Star Quality style.

Selecting Fragrance

The character of your fragrance is partly determined by your own personality. The ingredients of a perfume or cologne mesh with your individual body chemistry and smell a bit differently on you than on anyone else. Perfumes have a "top note," or the scent you detect when you sniff it in the bottle or first apply it to your skin; a "body," or an aroma which is the result of the perfume blending with your skin for two or three hours after you put it on; and a "dry out," or a lingering trace of the aroma that stays with you all day. Some perfumes have longer-lasting "dry outs" than others.

Because you should know what the "body" of the scent will be before you buy it, try it on at the perfume counter, then finish your shopping or have lunch while you let it mingle with your personal chemistry. If you still like the fragrance two hours later, buy it. Some perfumes, you will notice, begin to smell acrid or slightly stale on you, and some smell very strong; these do not work with your body type. Don't try on more than two scents at the same time; otherwise your nose will get confused by the blend of aromas.

If you are looking for a magnetic new fragrance but have no idea which of the hundreds that are available to choose, tell the salesperson the names of perfumes you've tried before and enjoyed. Perfumes are members of scent families—such as "floral scents," "citrusy scents," "mossy scents," "green scents," and sophisticated "Oriental" or "amber" scents. The family name means they are made with some of the same ingredients and have a similar effect. The experienced salesperson will know which family your past favorites came from, and can suggest others from the same family that will have a similar yet different aroma. You can also describe the "mood" you want your fragrance to create, or the time of day when you want to wear it.

Fragrances, no matter how fine, don't last forever, and some types self-destruct faster than others. Most perfumes tend to lose their true essence after a year or ten months. Because heat and air tend to deteriorate a perfume, store your scent in a cool place (even the refrigerator) and make sure you fasten the stopper tightly after each use. Aerosol or pump-type bottles are slightly more expensive but preserve the fragrance longer because they prevent air from entering. On the whole, perfumes last longer than colognes. No scent should be worn once it takes on an alcoholic or rancid aroma; use it in your bath instead of on your skin.

Other scent suggestions:

• If your skin is dry, an alcohol-based perfume or cologne may not last well on you. Try substituting a delicious-smelling bath oil, or a scented oil like patchouli, sandalwood, or musk. Remember, though many scented oils bear the same name, they are different brands; some are of a much finer quality than others. Try samples of different products before you select.

• You can choose a special fragrance and make it your trademark—a scent no one will smell again without thinking of you. You can also use perfumes and colognes as you would accessories, combining different fragrances with different clothes for different occasions.

• Don't discount a man's cologne. These spicy, woodsy fragrances work well with daytime business wear.

• The natural warmth from your body keeps perfume alive in the air around you. The joints of your body—the knees, wrists, elbows, and shoulders—are warm because they are always moving. Pulse points behind your ears are also warm. Don't spray your clothes or your hair with perfume—scent smells freshest and most subtle on your skin.

• You can bring your personal fragrance into your Star Quality surroundings by applying a small dab of your favorite oil or cologne to a lightbulb. When the light burns, the heat will spread your aroma throughout the room. I use more perfume on burning bulbs than I do on my body.

• Try layering scents. Apply just a touch to your wrists for daytime wear, then add additional layers behind your ears and knees, and to your cleavage for a dinner date or night on the town. You can also "layer" different scents and create your personal blend of perfume.

• Change your scent with the season. A light lavender water or eau de toilette in a floral scent will smell cooler on a hot summer night than the sophisticated, heady perfume you wear in the winter.

• For an unusual "dry perfume" with an East Indian echo, dab a touch of ground spice on your wrists and behind your earlobes. Try dried ginger, cinnamon, cardamom, or nutmeg, or create your own custom blend. Be sure the spices are fresh.

• A fine soap will give your body a faint, clean fragrance that may appeal to you more than perfume. Sachet makes an excellent perfume substitute, too. You can make your own by filling tiny satin pockets, or pouches made of veiling, with fine herbs and dried flowers like lavender, rosemary, roses, cloves, or a potpourri of sweet-smelling natural ingredients. Hang them in your closets and sprinkle them liberally throughout your drawers.

Never-Never Number One

Never overdo your aroma. Your scent should be an intimate part of you, and others shouldn't detect it down the block or in the room after you leave. I avoid some people because I simply can't take their overwhelming perfume but don't want to offend them by telling them so. Consider that scent is a personal preference; what smells heavenly to you may give someone else a migraine or ruin their appetite at the dinner table. Never wear perfume in a swimming pool or exercise class—this is not the time or the place for strong, sweet smells. Consideration for other peoples' noses is another reason you should take time to select the most delectable scent possible. Remember, too, that many of the cosmetic and grooming aids you use have strong scents of their own which may clash with your perfume. If you want to let a particular perfume fragrance identify you, try buying unscented cosmetics and deodorants, and use a mildly scented soap and shampoo.

HERITAGE SECRETS

Spicy-Sweet Breath

Your sweet breath is part of your unique aroma, too. Instead of using breath mints and medicinal-smelling sprays, try sweetening your breath the way the Ethiopian ladies do—by chewing on a stick of cinnamon. East Indians also sweeten their breath by chewing mixtures of spices after a meal. Try some delicious Indian fennel seeds for an unusual breath-sweetening taste that also helps the digestion.

A STAR QUALITY VOICE

Your voice is a tremendous part of your glamour. As all actors and actresses know, an impressive or interesting voice can steal all the attention in the room. I've always been thankful for my own deep, throaty contralto. The best way to learn how your voice sounds to others is to sneak up on yourself with a tape recorder; that is, turn it on when you're talking to someone and record yourself. When you listen to the tape, you may be in for some pleasant and unpleasant surprises as you hear the quality and tone of your own voice. Below are some suggestions for voice improvement:

• Reading aloud is a great way to improve your voice and your range of expression. Read to your children, or read your favorite poems and plays aloud to yourself and record your reading.

• Pay attention to your diction. Pronounce your words so that they are clearly understood. This is especially important for job interviews and business occasions; mumbling and jumbling never communicate a competent person. If you don't know how to pronounce a word, ask someone who does, or learn how to use the phonetic pronunciation guide of your dictionary. You can improve your diction by listening to yourself read or talk on a tape recorder, then practicing words you pronounced fuzzily.

• Practice using your voice to express different moods and emotions. Say the same sentence in efficient, romantic, enthusiastic, angry, or sad tones, and record the results.

• A speech and diction class or singing lessons may do far more to develop your Star Quality than a new coat or dress.

• A voice teacher once told me that the sound of your voice is inextricably related to the real you inside. A dynamic person, she said, will usually have a dynamic voice; a sad or depressed person may have a flat, uninteresting voice. You may have to do some serious self-analysis to really change the way you sound. Consider that changing your voice may be the first step to changing the inner you.

• A lady with Star Quality knows not only how to talk but how to listen, too. No matter how much you love the sound of your own voice, when other people talk, really listen. Let everything about your face, eyes, and body show that you're giving them your complete and full attention. Make an effort to remember what other people say and refer to it in your conversations. This is guaranteed to make you the best-loved person in the world.

STAR QUALITY GRACE

To be really beautiful, you must move, stand, and sit with the authoritative, eye-catching grace of an important person. Because we never actually see ourselves moving, it's easy to remain oblivious to our body language. Try to catch yourself unawares. Notice how you look when you walk by a department store window. Are you slouching along with your shoulders hunched and your stomach poked out? If so, then this is the way you probably walk most of the time. Check yourself once an hour when you're sitting in a restaurant, theater, or at your desk. Is your back rounded? (If so, it's working on forming a permanent dowager's hump.) Try to monitor the way you are standing at a party, and ask yourself what your folded arms, clenched hands, or careless stance are telling other people about you. Look at yourself in an informal photograph. How are you standing? Ask a good friend to evaluate your posture and imitate the way you walk. (This may be painful; be sure to ask a *good* friend.) Once you've obtained a mental picture of how you move, stand, or sit, conscientiously set about to improve your posture, walking with your stomach in and held up, your back straight and shoulders down, and your neck stretched up and chin in. Classes in the martial arts, ballet, or modern dance are bound to improve your posture while they give you some good figure-fixin' exercise.

STAR QUALITY ATTITUDE

For years I've led a busy, active life, filled with the usual number of disappointments and joys. There are mornings when I get out of bed and I'm down. I feel that I am a very unattractive person—inside and outside, too. Yet I know that no matter how I feel about myself, in less than an hour I'm going to have to put myself together, rush off to an early appointment, and present the most beautiful version of Barbara to the world. I know I will have to be not only attractive but pleasant and competent, too. These are the mornings I find it most important to take a moment for my personal meditation—a meditation I've been practicing every day of my life for years. I call it "reidentifying myself with me." I get out of bed, look at my fingers, my legs, and my arms, and then I look at my face in the mirror. I put my head out the window, take a deep breath of cool, morning air, and say, "Thank God I'm alive today. Thank God I'm still breathing and everything on me is still moving." After that, my mood inevitably improves. I know I will go to my dressing table and work to bring out my most elegant self. I think about what I have to do that day and the impression I want to make, and I prepare myself inwardly for the challenge ahead. I consider the different personalities I have to deal with and plan a strategy to handle them. Then I think of the events in my day I am bound to enjoy. When I leave my house, I know that my efforts to be beautiful will succeed.

I believe that every woman should have a personal technique for identifying herself and gathering together the forces that enable her to be as beautiful as she wants to be. This invisible attitude, more than anything else you can do, creates Star Quality.

INDEX

acne, 30–33
  black skin and, 31
  cure of, 31
  diet and, 32–33
  home remedy for, 32
  keloid scarring from, 35
  nature and causes of, 29, 30–31
aerobic exercise, 27, 30
African wrap, 164
Afro hairstyle, 101–102
age:
  makeup related to, 50
  skin and, 17, 25, 26
alcohol, rubbing, in astringents, 23
allergies, 29, 148
androgen, acne and, 31
ashy skin, 36–37
astringents:
  Barbados daiquiri, 23
  for enlarged pores, 38
  kitchen, 23
attitude, star quality, 201

baby oil, as cleansing cream, 18, 19
Bacon, Jim, 4
balding, 141
Balinese gold fingers, 184
Barbara Walden Complete Makeup, *see*
    Makeup, Barbara Walden Complete
bath oil, fragrant Indian, 45
baths:
  Barbara Walden luxury, 44
  Cleopatra milk, 44
  dry-skin, 45
  flake-removing rub before, 46
  Japanese-style ache-relieving, 45
beauty, importance to black women of,
  11

beauty contests, black girls in, 4
beauty marks, 81–82
belts, 162
benzoyl peroxide, 31
blackheads, 30, 31
"black is beautiful," 1, 48
black skin, beauty of, 15
black women:
  cosmetics designed for, 48–49
  cosmetics market represented by, 49
  1980's look for, 49–50
  style of, 142
bleaching creams, 189
  dehydrated skin and, 38
  testing of, 34
blemishes, concealing of, 83
Blistex, 71
blood vessels, 26
body, *see* figure
Bororo women, 108
Bradley, Ethel, 7
braided hair, 103–105
  maintaining of, 103–104
  removing braids, 104–105
  removing ornaments before sleep, 105
  slack vs. tight, 105
  taming of, 105
  universal beauty of, 104
breast cancer, 168
breath, spicy-sweet, 199
brewers' yeast, 28
brown spots, bleaching of, 189

caffeine, 168
  skin affected by, 27, 37
calcium supplements, 27
carbohydrates, refined, 166–167
Carmen Jones, 3

Carson, Pirie, Scott, and Company, 9–10
Car Wash, 4
castor oil:
　for bath, 45
　bleaching brown spots with, 189
　as cleansing cream, 18
　for hair, 130
Cele women, 104, 111
cells, dead, 20, 25
Chap Stick, 71
chignon hairstyle, 102–103
circles beneath eyes, 69–70, 76
cleansers, abrasive, 20
cleansing creams, kitchen products as,
　18–19
cleansing lotions, water soluble, 18
Cleopatra (film), 3, 4
Cleopatra eyes, 66
Clift, Montgomery, 2
clothes, 142–174
　accessories and, 161–165
　black women and, 142
　bleaching of, 156
　budget and, 151–152
　care of, 154–157
　color choices in, 145
　construction of, 150–151
　"dry clean only" (DCOs), 155, 156
　dry cleaner and, 154
　fabric choices in, 146–148
　fading of, 147–148
　fashion weaknesses and, 152
　fit and cut of, 148–150
　ironing of, 156
　as irregulars, 148
　last-minute shopping for, 153
　laundering of, 155–156
　leather, care of, 157
　other people's fashion images and,
　　153
　pilling of, 148
　in preselected costumes, 160–161
　price vs. appearance of, 153–154
　recombining colors and silhouettes of,
　　159–160
　recycling of, 161
　role playing and, 143
　shopping tips for, 143–154
　shrinking of, 147
　skin affected by, 148
　stains on, 154, 155
　storing of, 157
　study of style and, 144–145
　in wardrobe makeover, 157–165
　wrinkling of, 147
compress rehydration treatment, 38
concealers, 69–70, 76
conditioners, 125–131
　African butter, 130

after-shampoo rinse-away, 126
Caribbean coconut sun, 136
hair-building, 127–128
homemade mayonnaise protein,
　128–129
hot oil-conditioning treatment, 127
myths about, 130
potent guacamole, 129
protein, 128–129
rosemary highlight, 129
sleek almond oil, 127
sweet olive oil, 127–128
thyme herbal rinse, 126
vinegar rinse, 126
constipation, skin care and, 26–27
contour shading, 57–59
　selecting product for, 57
　technique for, 57–59
cosmetics, "natural" ingredients in, 29
coverup for under-eye circles, 69–70, 76
cream rouge, 59–60
　application of, 59–60
　selecting product, 59
curling irons, 107, 109
cuticle nippers, 177

dandruff, 139–140
dark patches, concealing of, 83
Dazzle Look, 77–82
　beauty marks for, 81–82
　blush for, 80
　contouring for, 78
　extra touches for, 80–82
　eyes for, 79
　foundation for, 78
　glitter for, 80–81
　hairline color for, 81
　lashes for, 79–80
　lip color for, 80
　powder for, 79
　rouge for, 79
dehydrated skin, 37–38
depilatories, 46, 47
dermabrasion, black skin and, 31
dermatologists:
　acne treated by, 31, 32
　black skin and, 32
dermatosis papulosa nigra, 34–35
diet (eating habits):
　acne and, 32–33
　avoiding huge quantities in, 168
　for hair care, 133–134
　for nails, 185
　three months without junk food, 33
diets (weight-reduction), 165–169
　crash, 169
　moderation in, 168
　wrinkles and sags caused by, 40
"double press," 109

drugs, skin affected by, 27
dry cleaning, 154, 155, 156

exzema, 28
Egyptian almond scrub, 20, 21
Egyptian body glitter, sexy, 81
Egyptian lips, 74
electrolysis, 47
Etruscan women, 108
exercises:
  aerobic, 27, 30
  in Barbara's "Too Busy to Exercise"
    System, 169–171
  for complexion tone, 42
  facial, 30, 41–43
  invisible, practice of, 171
  kitchen calisthentics, 170
  neck-relaxing, 42
  for puffy eyes, 41
  reaching, stretching, bending, 170
  walking, 169–170
eyebrow pencils, 62, 63, 64
eyebrow shaping, 61–62
  with pencil, 62
  with razor blade (suicidal), 62
  with tweezer, 61–62
eye color, 62–67
  in Barbara's Natural Look, 76
  blending of, 67
  for Egyptian lips, 74
  eye lining and, 64
  kohl, 65
  selecting colors, 63–64
  selecting product, 63
  shadowing lid, 65–67
  tools for, 64
eyelashes, 67–69
  application of, 79–80
  curling and straightening, 69
  in Dazzle Look, 79–80
  false, 69
  glues for, 80
  lengthener, homemade, 68
eyelids:
  disguising heavy folds of, 87
  shadowing of, 65–67
eye-makeup-remover, mineral oil as, 19
eyes:
  Cleopatra, 66
  close-set, 86
  concealing circles beneath, 69–70, 76
  deep-set, 86
  flat, 87
  mascara in, 68
  perfecting shape of, 85–87
  protruding, 85–86
  puffy, 40–41
  small, 86

wide-set, 87
wrinkles around, 40

face:
  hairstyle and shape of, 96–97
  improving shape of, 83–84
  redesigning of, 82–87
  shape of, 51–52, 57–59
  shaving of, 46
face powder, 60–61
  application of, 60–61
  puff for, 60
  selection of, 60
facials:
  carrot soufflé icy refining, 43
  exotic Asian, 28
  hydrating, 37–38
  nightbird, 41–43
  oil-blotting, 24
  once-a-week deep-cleansing, 21
  pore-shrinking, 39
  smoothie ash-banishing, 20, 36–37
  West African pumpkin-seed, 22
  see also masques
fats, saying no to, 167
fatty acids, for hair care, 134
figure (body):
  big, 172–173
  camouflaging flaws in, 174
  girdle recommended for, 171–172
  hairstyle and, 97–98
  illusion as aid to, 172–174
  short, 173
  short-waisted, 174
  slim and in-shape, 165–174
  tall, 173–174
  thin, 173
folic acid, 28
folliculitis, 130
foot care, 189–192
  Princess Pedicure for, 190–192
foot massage, Japanese, 191
footwear, 149–150, 161–162
foundation, 53–57
  application of, 56–57
  in Barbara's Natural Look, 76
  in Complete Makeup, 53–54
  oil- vs. water-based, 55–56
  skin tones and, 54–55
  testing on skin, 54
  texture of, 56
fragrance, star quality, 196–199
Frank, Marvin, 8–9
fresheners, lemon, 19–20
fried foods, saying no to, 167
Fula tribe, 78

gelatin, as nail-builder, 185–186
girdles, value of, 171–172

glamour, investing in, 12–13
glitter, 80–81
glues, eyelash, 80
grace, star quality, 200–201

hair, 88–141
  abnormal growth of, 48
  Afro, 101–102
  basic care of, 123–141
  black, as delicate, 90–91
  black women's, 88
  blow-dry and curl, 106–107
  braided, 103–105
  brushing of, 132
  castor oil for, 130–131
  changing times and, 89–90
  chignon, 102–103
  coloring of, 118–123
  combing of, 132–133
  cornrowing of, 103, 104
  curly ("reverse") perm, 114–117
  curly-perm look alternatives, 116
  cutting at home, 99–100
  cutting to condition, 99
  damaged, cutting of, 98
  dandruff and, 139–140
  destroyed by straightening, 110
  diet for, 133–134
  double-permed, 110–111
  dry, brittle, 135–136
  enjoying change of style, 94
  face shape and, 96–97
  fatty acids for, 134
  figure and, 97–98
  finding "doctor" for, 91–95
  freedom of style for, 89
  good vs. bad, 88–89
  gray, dying of, 119–120
  gray, henna on, 120–121
  graying of, 140
  henna, 120–123
  henna, do-it-yourself, 121–123
  home care for curly perms, 116–117
  home perm for, 111–114
  hot-combing of, 108–109
  kinky, 101–102, 105, 106–107, 110,
    125, 130
  length of neck and, 97
  limp, lifeless, 137–138
  long, growing of, 100–101
  loss of (balding), 141
  natural texture of, 101–105
  oily, formerly dry or normal, 138–139
  ornamenting of, 105, 108
  permanent dyes for, 119
  permed, caring for, 114
  porous, 136–137
  precision-cut, 98
  professional perm for, 111

protein in diet for, 133–134
  from relaxed to natural, 105–106
  relaxing traditions and, 111
  relaxing with chemicals, 109
  relaxing with heat, 106–109
  scalp massage for, 131
  shampooing of, see shampoo
  short, as beautiful, 101
  style guidelines for, 95–98
  sweet-scented, 124
  taming snarls in, 133
  touch-ups after chemical straightening
    of, 110–111
  troubleshooting guide for care of,
    134–141
  washing with soap, 124
  wigs, 117–118
hairline color, 81
hair removal, 46–47
  depilatories for, 46, 47
  by electrolysis, 47
  by shaving, 46
  smoothing skin with, 46
  by waxing, 46–47
hair stylists:
  in big city, 95
  communicating your personal style to,
    93–94
  disappointment with, 94
  honesty with, 93
  learning from, 95
  preparing for first appointment with,
    92
  selecting of, 91–92
  talking to, 92–93
half shoulder stand, 42
hands, 175–189
  bleaching brown spots on, 189
  smoothing "facial" for, 189
  touchworthy, 188
hats, 162
head rolls, 42
heating system, skin condition and, 17,
  37
herbal teas, 27
  for hydrating facials, 37–38
Heritage Secrets:
  African Butter Conditioner, 130
  African Way With Jewels, The, 165
  African Wrap, The, 164
  Balinese Gold Fingers, 184
  Barbados Daiquiri Astringent, 23
  Beauty of Kohl, The, 65
  Caribbean Coconut Sun Conditioner,
    136
  Caribbean Colors, 160
  Cleopatra Eyes, 66
  Cleopatra's Cleanser, 19
  Egyptian Almond Scrub, 21

Egyptian Bread Masque, 25
Egyptian Lips, 74
Exotic Asian Facial, 28
Food for the Hair, 133
Fragrant Indian Bath Oil, 45
Japanese Foot Massage, 191
Moroccan Henna Wrap for Problem
    Nails, 186
North African Henna Masque, 39
Ornamenting the Hair, 108
Posture Improvement, 171
Relaxing Traditions, 111
Sexy Egyptian Body Glitter, 81
Special Makeup From Africa, 78
Spicy-Sweet Breath, 199
Sweet-Scented Hair, 124
Universal Beauty of Braids, The, 104
West African Pumpkin-seed Facial, 22
hormones, acne and, 31
hyperpigmentation, 32, 33–34, 47

Japanese women, 133
jewelry, 164–165
junk foods, acne and, 32–33

keloids, 35–36
Kennedy, John F., 4
kohl, 65
Korean women, 133

laundering, 155–156
leather items, care of, 157
LeClair, Donna, 185
lion face (exercise), 43
lip care, 71
lip color, 70–74
    in Barbara's Natural Look, 77
    in Dazzle Look, 80
    lip liners and, 71–72
    preparing lips for, 70–71
lip gloss, perils of, 73
lip liners, 71–72
    selection of, 72–73
    technique for, 72
lips, improving shape of, 85
lipstick brushes, 73–74
lipsticks:
    designing own shades of, 73
    selection of, 72
    technique for, 74
    texture of, 73
    tools for, 73–74
lovemaking, skin affected by, 27

Magnin, Joseph, department store, 8–9
makeup, 48–87
    African-style, 78
    age and, 50
    as art, 51

dazzle, see Dazzle Look
evening, 51
going to bed with, 17
1980's look in, 49–50
professional makeup artist and, 53
removal of, 17–18
shape of face and, 51–52
Makeup, Barbara Walden Complete,
    50–75
    clean, moisturized skin for, 52
    concealing circles beneath the eyes in,
        69–70
    contour shading in, 57–59
    cream rouge in, 59–61
    essentials for, 51–53
    eyebrow shaping in, 61–62
    eye color in, 62–67
    face powder in, 60–61
    foundation in, 53–57
    lip color in, 70–74
    mascara in, 67–69
    powder blush in, 75
    right light for, 52
    selecting products for, 53, 54
    sketching face for, 51–52
    ten steps of, 53–75
makeup, Natural Look, see Natural
    Look, Barbara's Six-Step
Mali shawl, 163
manicure, home, 175–180
    base coat applied, 178
    drying polish, 180
    enamel applied, 178–179
    removing old polish, 177
    selecting nail enamel, 179
    shaping nails, 177
    smoothing cuticles, 177
    soaking and cleaning nails, 178
    tools for, 176
    top coat applied, 179–180
    see also nails
mascara, 67–69
    application of, 68
    in eyes, 68
    selecting product, 67–68
    see also eyelashes
masques:
    avocado smash, 22
    bran and yogurt, 20, 22
    Egyptian bread, 25
    grandmother's egg-on-the-face, 22
    North African henna, 39
    see also facials
mayonnaise, as cleansing cream, 18
medications:
    hair growth and, 47
    skin affected by, 29
melanin stains, 20
melanocytes, 34

menopause, excess hair and, 47
menstrual periods, 31
Micks, Ralph Holbrook, 108
milk bath, 44
mineral oil, as eye-makeup remover, 19
moisturizers:
    dehydration and, 37
    dry-skin, 24
    sun-protection, 29
moles, removing hair from, 47
Morris, Barbara, 106, 127–128

nail enamel:
    application of, 178
    chipped, 179
    selection of, 179
    see also manicure, home
nail extension, 180–183
    easy nail sculpture, 182
    quick party-time, 181
nails:
    dazzle-time touches for, 183–184
    diet for, 185–186
    easily broken, 185
    glamicure for, 186–187
    Moroccan henna wrap for, 186
    protection of, 183
    ragged, rough, uneven, 187–188
    rigid, splitting, peeling, 184–185
    stained or yellowish, 187
    troubleshooting guide for care of,
        134–141
    wrapping and capping of, 183
Natural Look, Barbara's Six-Step (I-hate-
    to-Wear-Makeup Look), 75–77
    coverup for under-eye circles, 76
    eye color in, 76
    foundation in, 76
    lip color in, 77
    powder blush in, 77
    powder in, 76
"natural" look, waning popularity of,
    49–50

oil glands, 26, 30
oils, exotic, 24
overwashing, 18

PABA, 29
pimples, 30, 31, 32
pores:
    enlarged, 38–39
    heavy creams and, 24
post-inflammatory hyperpigmentation
    (PIHP), 33–34
posture improvement, 171
powder blush, 75
    in Barbara's Natural Look, 77
Private Lives of Adam and Eve, The, 4

protein:
    conditioners, 128–129
    for hair health, 133–134
    as skin food, 27–28
psoriasis, 28, 34, 139
puffy eyes, 40–41
pumice stones, 46
purses, 163

Raeburn, Dan, 6, 9
Raintree County, 2–3
Roman women, 108
Rooney, Mickey, 4, 5
rubs, flake-removing, 46

salt, avoidance of, 168
Satan's Seven Sinners, 4–5
scalp, massaging of, 131
scarring, black skin and, 31, 32, 35
scarves, 163
scrubs:
    cornmeal and buttermilk, 20
    Egyptian almond, 20, 21
    seborrheic dermatitis, 139
self-love, essential, 11–12
Senegalese bead belt, 163
sesame oil, 29, 45
shampoo, 123–125
    for dry hair, 123
    frequency of, 125
    myths about, 124–125
    for oily hair, 123
    recommended method of, 125
    with soap, 124
shaving body hair, 46
shawls, 163
shoe polishes, 157
shoes, fitting of, 149–150
showers:
    as circulation bracers, 46
    sour cream, 45
skin:
    age and, 17, 25, 26
    allergies and, 29, 148
    all-skin-type cleansing program for,
        17–18
    ashy, 36–37
    black, beauty of, 15
    "combination," 17, 23
    concealing of, 83
    covering flaws in, 83
    dehydrated, 37
    dry, 16, 18, 24, 29, 45
    flaky, 16–17
    glamorous, tips for, 25–30
    most common problems of, 30–42
    myths about, 16–17
    nourishment for, 27–29

oily, 16–17, 18, 23, 52
   typecasting of, 16–17
skin cancer, 29
skin care, 15–47
   all-body, 44–47
   high priority of, 15–16
   see also specific problems and treat-
      ments
skin diseases, prevention of, 28, 83
skin tones, selecting foundation and,
      54–55
sleep:
   complexion and, 27
   puffy eyes and, 40–41
sleeping pills, 27
smoking, skin affected by, 27
soap:
   avoidance of, 18
   dehydrated skin and, 37
sponges, polyester-fiber, 20
squinting, lines around eyes from, 40
star quality, 193–201
   in attitude, 201
   in fragrance, 196–197
   in grace, 200–201
   in surroundings, 195–196
   in voice, 199–200
stoles, 163
stratum corneum, 20
sugar, saying no to, 166
sun exposure, skin affected by, 29, 40
sunscreens, 29
Swazi people, 111

Taylor, Elizabeth, 2–3
Thrifty Drug Stores, 7–8
tissues, misuse of, 20
tofu (bean curd), in facial, 28
towel, pillowcase covered with, 20
traction alopecia, 105
tweezing, 61–62

Vaseline petroleum jelly, 18, 71, 189
   as skin rejuvenator, 25
vegetable oil:
   as cleansing cream, 18
   in diet, 28–29
   as skin food, 28
Vitamin A, 28
   for hair, 134
   tonic toner, 28
voice, star quality, 199–200

Walden, Barbara:
   in Chicago success, 9–10
   cosmetics business started by, 6–8
   custom-made foundation of, 6
   in Hollywood, 2–5
   in major career decision, 8–9
   in modeling school, 1–2
   in nightclub job, 2
   present activities of, 10–11
walking, as exercise, 169–170
walnut oil, as makeup removing
      cleanser, 19
water, drinking, skin care and, 26, 37
water, mineral, spritzing face with, 37
weather, skin condition and, 17, 37
wigs, 117–118
   selection of, 117–118
   wear and care of, 118
wraps, 163
wrinkles, 39–40
   causes of, summarized, 39–40
   "happy" lines as, 40
   heavy night creams and, 24
   stretching skin and, 29–30

yoga posture, 42

Zulu women, 108

About the Authors

Barbara Walden was born in Camden, N.J., and established her first career in Hollywood as a young dancer and actress. She appeared in such films as *What a Way to Go, The Ten Commandments,* and *Night of the Quarter Moon.* There she experienced the problems black women had in finding suitable makeup and hair products. As a result, she began developing cosmetics that were right for her and eventually built up her own cosmetics company. Her products now appear in leading department stores in the United States and abroad. In addition to running her Los Angeles-based firm, she travels extensively, bringing her "black is beautiful" message to drug rehabilitation centers, mental hospitals, schools, and groups of senior citizens.

Vicki Lindner is a free-lance writer whose articles and fiction have appeared in many magazines. She has collaborated on several books in the fields of health and beauty.